Book 5

———◆◆◆———

MAXIMIZE YOUR POTENTIAL
THROUGH THE POWER OF
YOUR SUBCONSCIOUS MIND
FOR A

More Spiritual Life

———◆◆◆———

Other Hay House Classics Titles by Dr. Joseph Murphy

Believe in Yourself
Miracles of Your Mind
Techniques in Prayer Therapy

Other Books in the MAXIMIZE YOUR POTENTIAL Series:

Book 1: *Maximize Your Potential Through the
Power of Your Subconscious Mind to Overcome Fear and Worry*

———

Book 2: *Maximize Your Potential Through the Power of
Your Subconscious Mind to Create Wealth and Success*

———

Book 3: *Maximize Your Potential Through the Power of Your
Subconscious Mind to Develop Self-Confidence and Self-Esteem*

———

Book 4: *Maximize Your Potential Through the
Power of Your Subconscious Mind for Health and Vitality*

———

Book 6: *Maximize Your Potential Through the
Power of Your Subconscious Mind for an Enriched Life*

⊞✝⊞ ⊞✝⊞ ⊞✝⊞

Book 5

MAXIMIZE YOUR POTENTIAL
THROUGH THE POWER OF
YOUR SUBCONSCIOUS MIND
FOR A
More Spiritual Life

One of a Series of Six Books
by
Dr. Joseph Murphy

Edited and Updated for the 21st Century
by Arthur R. Pell, Ph.D.

HAY HOUSE, INC.
Carlsbad, California • New York City
London • Sydney • Johannesburg
Vancouver • Hong Kong • New Delhi

DR. JOSEPH MURPHY

Maximize Your Potential Through the Power of Your Subconscious Mind for a More Spiritual Life is one of a series of six books by Joseph Murphy, D.D., Ph.D., edited and updated for the 21st century by Arthur R. Pell, Ph.D. Copyright © 2005 The James A. Boyer Revocable Trust. Exclusive worldwide rights in all languages available only through JMW Group Inc.

Published and distributed in the United States by: Hay House, Inc.: www.hayhouse. com • **Published and distributed in Australia by:** Hay House Australia Pty. Ltd.: www. hayhouse.com.au • **Published and distributed in the United Kingdom by:** Hay House UK, Ltd.: www.hayhouse.co.uk • **Published and distributed in the Republic of South Africa by:** Hay House SA (Pty), Ltd.: www.hayhouse.co.za • **Distributed in Canada by:** Raincoast: www.raincoast.com • **Published in India by:** Hay House Publishers India: www.hayhouse.co.in

Design: Nick Welch

Library of Congress Cataloging-in-Publication Data

Murphy, Joseph, 1898-1981
  Maximize your potential through the power of your subconscious mind for a more spiritual life / Joseph Murphy; edited and updated for the 21st century by Arthur R. Pell. -- 1st Hay House ed.
     p. cm.
  ISBN-13: 978-1-4019-1218-5 (tradepaper) 1. Spiritual life. 2. Spirituality. I. Pell, Arthur R. II. Title.
  BL624.M863 2008
  299'.93--dc22

                          2006037925

ISBN: 978-1-4019-1218-5

11 10 09 08   4 3 2 1
1st Hay House edition, August 2008

Printed in the United States of America

CONTENTS

Introduction to the Series

*W*ake up and live! No one is destined to be unhappy or consumed with fear and worry, live in poverty, suffer ill health, and feel rejected and inferior. God created all humans in His image and has given us the power to overcome adversity and attain happiness, harmony, health, and prosperity.

You have within you the power to enrich your life! How to do this is no secret. It has been written about and practiced for millennia. You will find it in the works of the ancient philosophers, and all of the great religions have preached about it. It is in the Hebrew scriptures, the Christian Gospels, Greek philosophy, the Muslim Koran, the Buddhist sutras, the Hindu Bhagavad Gita, and the writings of Confucius and Lao Tse. You will also find it in the works of modern psychologists and theologians.

This is the basis of the philosophy of Dr. Joseph Murphy, one of the great inspirational writers and lecturers of the 20th century. He was not just a clergyman, but also a major figure in the modern interpretation of scriptures and other religious writings. As minister-director of the Church of Divine Science in Los Angeles, his lectures and sermons were attended by 1,300 to 1,500 people every Sunday, and millions tuned in to his daily radio program. He wrote more than 30 books, and his most well-known one, *The Power of the Unconscious Mind,* was first published in 1963 and became an immediate bestseller. It was acclaimed as one of the greatest self-help guides ever written. Millions of copies have, and continue to be, sold all over the world.

Following the success of this book, Dr. Murphy lectured to audiences of thousands in several countries. In his lectures he pointed out how real people have radically improved their lives by applying specific aspects of his concepts, and he provided practical guidelines on how all people can enrich themselves.

Dr. Murphy was a proponent of the New Thought movement, which was developed in the late 19th and early 20th centuries by many philosophers and deep thinkers who studied it and preached, wrote, and practiced a new way of looking at life. By combining metaphysical, spiritual, and pragmatic approaches to the way we think and live, they uncovered the secret for attaining what we truly desire.

This philosophy wasn't a religion in the traditional sense, but it was based on an unconditional belief in a higher being, an eternal presence: God. It was called by various names, such as "New Thought" and "New Civilization."

The proponents of New Thought or New Civilization preached a fresh idea of life that makes use of methods that lead to perfected results. They based their thinking on the concept that the human soul is connected with the atomic mind of universal substance, which links our lives with the universal law of supply, and we have the power to use it to enrich our lives. To achieve our goals, we must work, and through this work we may suffer the thorns and heartaches of humankind. We can do all these things only as we have found the law and worked out an understanding of the principles that God seemed to have written in riddles in the past.

The New Thought concept can be summed up in these words:

You can become what you want to be.

All that we achieve and all that we fail to achieve is the direct result of our own thoughts. In a just and ordered universe, where loss of balance would mean total destruction, individual responsibility must be absolute. Our purity, impurity, weaknesses, and strengths are ours alone. They are brought about by ourselves and not by another. They can only be altered by ourselves, and never by anyone else. All of our happiness and suffering evolve from within. As we think, so we are; as we continue to think, so we remain. The only way we can rise, conquer, and achieve is by lifting up our thoughts. The only reason we may remain weak, abject, and miserable is to *refuse* to elevate our minds.

All achievements—whether in the business, intellectual, or spiritual world—are the result of definitely directed thought; and are governed by the same law and are reached by the same method. The only difference lies in the object of attainment. Those who would accomplish little must sacrifice little; those who would achieve much must sacrifice much; those who would attain a great deal must sacrifice a great deal.

New Thought means a new life: a way of living that is healthier, happier, and more fulfilling in every possible manner and expression.

Actually, there is nothing new in this, for it is as old and time-honored as humankind. It is novel to us when we discover the truths of life that set us free from lack, limitation, and unhappiness. At that moment, New Thought becomes a recurring, expanding awareness of the creative power within; of mind-principle; and of our Divine potential to be, do, and express more of our individual and natural abilities, aptitudes, and talents. The central mind-principle is that new thoughts, ideas, attitudes, and beliefs create new conditions. According to our beliefs, is it done unto us—good, bad, or indifferent. The essence of New Thought consists of the continual renewing of our mind, that we may manifest what is good, acceptable, and the perfect will of God.

To prove is to know surely, and to have trustworthy knowledge and experience. The truths of New Thought are practical, easy to demonstrate, and within the realm of accomplishment of everyone—if and when he or she chooses. All that is required is an open mind and a willing heart: open to hearing old truths presented in a different way; willing to change and to relinquish outmoded beliefs and to accept unfamiliar ideas and concepts—to have a higher vision of life, or a healing presence within.

The rebirth of our mind constitutes the entire purpose and practice of New Thought. Without this ongoing daily renewal, there can be no change. New Thought establishes and realizes an entirely new attitude and consciousness that inspires and enables us to enter into "life more abundant."

We have within us limitless powers to choose and to decide, and complete freedom to be conformed or to be transformed. To be conformed is to live according to that which already has taken or been given form—that which is visible and apparent to our own senses, including the ideas, opinions, beliefs, and edicts of others. It is to live and to be governed "by the fleeting and unstable fashions and conditions of the moment." The very word *conformed* suggests that our present environment has shape, and that we do not and should not deny its existence. All around us there are injustices, improprieties, and inequalities. We may and do find ourselves involved in them at times, and we should face them with courage and honesty and do our best to resolve them with the integrity and intelligence that we now possess.

Generally, the world accepts and believes that our environment is the cause of our present condition and circumstance—and the usual reaction and tendency is to drift into a state of acquiescence and quiet acceptance of the present. This is conformity of the worst kind: the consciousness of defeatism. It's worse because it is self-imposed. It is giving all power and attention to the outer, manifested state. New Thought insists on the renewal of the mind, and the recognition and acknowledgment of our responsibility in life—our ability to respond to the truths we now know.

One of the most active and effective of New Thought teachers, Charles Fillmore, co-founder of the Unity School of Christianity, was a firm believer in personal responsibility. In his book

The Revealing Word, he wrote (simply, and without equivocation): "Our consciousness is our real environment. The outer environment is always in correspondence to our consciousness."

Anyone who is open and willing to accept the responsibility has begun the transformation—the renewal of the mind that enables us to participate in our transformed life. "To transform" is "to change from one condition or state to another" (which is qualitatively better and more fulfilling) "from lack to abundance; loneliness to companionship; limitation to fullness; illness to vibrant health"—through this indwelling wisdom and power, the healing presence will remain within.

True and granted, there are some things we cannot change: the movement of the planets, the turn of the seasons, the pull of the oceans and tides, and the apparent rising and setting of the sun. Neither can we alter the minds and thoughts of another person— but we can change ourselves.

Who can prevent or inhibit the movement of your imagination and will? Only you can give that power to another. You can be transformed by the renewing of your mind. This is the key to a new life. You're a recording machine; and all the beliefs, impressions, opinions, and ideas accepted by you are impressed in your deeper subconscious. But you can change. You can begin now to fill your mind with noble and Godlike patterns of thoughts, and align yourself with the infinite spirit within. Claim beauty, love, peace, wisdom, creative ideas . . . and the infinite will respond accordingly, transforming your mind, body, and circumstances. Your thought is the medium between your spirit, your body, and the material world.

The transformation begins as we meditate, think upon, and absorb into our mentality those qualities that we desire to experience and express. Theoretical knowledge is good and necessary. We should understand what we're doing and why. However, actual change depends entirely on stirring up the gifts within—the invisible and intangible spiritual power given fully to every one of us.

This, and only this, ultimately breaks up and dissolves the very real claims and bondage of past unhappiness and distress. In addition, it heals the wounds of heartbreak and emotional pain. We all desire and require peace of mind—the greatest gift—in order to bring it into our environment. Mentally and emotionally, contemplate Divine peace, filling our mind and heart, our entire being. First say, "Peace be unto this house."

To contemplate lack of peace, disharmony, unhappiness, and discord, and expect peace to manifest is to expect the apple seed to grow into a pear. It makes little or no sense, and it violates all sense of reason, but it is the way of the world. We must seek ways to change our minds—to repent where necessary. As a result, renewal will occur, following naturally. It is desirable and necessary to transform our lives by ceasing to conform to the world's way of choosing or deciding, according to the events already formed and manifested.

The word *metaphysical* has become a synonym for the modern, organized movement. It was first used by Aristotle. Considered by some to have been his greatest writing, his 13th volume was simply entitled *Metaphysics*. The dictionary definition is: "Beyond natural science; the science of pure being." *Meta-* means "above, or beyond." *Metaphysics,* then, means "above or beyond physics"—"above or beyond the physical," the world of form. "Meta" is above that; it is the spirit of the mind, which is behind all things.

Biblically, the spirit of God is good. "They that worship God worship the spirit, or truth." When we have the spirit of goodness, truth, beauty, love, and goodwill, it is actually the Divine in us, moving through us. God, truth, life, energy, spirit—can it not be defined? How can it be? "To define it is to limit it."

This is expressed in a beautiful old meditation:

Ever the same in my innermost being: eternal, absolutely one, whole, complete, perfect; I AM indivisible, timeless, shapeless, ageless—without face, form, or figure. I AM the silent brooding presence, fixed in the hearts of all men (and women).

We must believe and accept that whatever we imagine and feel to be true will come to pass; whatever we desire for another, we are wishing for ourselves.

Emerson wrote: "We become what we think about all day long." In other words and most simply stated: Spirit, thought, mind, and meta is the expression of creative presence and power—and as in nature (physical laws), any force can be used two ways. For example, water can clean us or drown us; electricity can make life easier or more deadly. The Bible says: "I form the light, and create darkness; I make peace, and evil; I, the Lord, do all these things— I wound, I heal; I bless, I curse."

No angry deity is punishing us; we punish ourselves by misuse of the mind. We also are blessed (benefited) when we comprehend this fundamental principle and presence, and learn and accept a new thought or an entire concept.

Metaphysics, then, is the study of causation—concerned not with the effect that is now manifest, but rather with that which is causing the result. This discipline approaches spiritual ideas as scientists approach the world of form, just as they investigate the mind or causation from which the visible is formed, or derived. If a mind is changed, or a cause is changed, the effect is changed.

The strength and beauty of metaphysics, in my opinion, is that it is not confined to any one particular creed, but is universal. One can be a Jew, Christian, Muslim, or Buddhist and yet still be a metaphysician.

There are poets, scientists, and philosophers who claim no creed; their belief is metaphysical.

Jesus was a master metaphysician—he understood the mind and employed it to lift up, inspire, and heal others.

When Mahatma Gandhi (the "great-souled" one) was asked what his religion was, he replied, "I am a Christian . . . a Jew . . . a Buddhist . . . a Hindu . . . I AM all these things."

The term *New Thought* has become a popular, generalized term. Composed of a very large number of churches, centers, prayer

groups, and institutions, this has become a metaphysical movement that reveals the oneness or unity of humankind with infinite
life . . . with the innate dignity, worth, or value of every individual.
In fact, and in truth, the emphasis is on the individual rather than
on an organizational body or function. But as mentioned, there is
nothing new in New Thought. Metaphysics is actually the oldest
of all religious approaches. It reveals our purpose to express God,
and the greater measures of the Good: "I AM come to bring you
life and that more abundantly." It reveals our identity: "children
of the infinite" who are loved and have spiritual value as necessary
parts of the Creative Holy (whole) One.

Metaphysics enables and assists us to return to our Divine
Source, and ends the sense of separation and feeling of alienation; of wandering in a barren, unfriendly desert wasteland. This
approach has always been, is now, and ever will be available to
all—patiently waiting our discovery and revelation.

Many thousands have been introduced to New Thought
through one or another of its advocates. Its formation was gradual,
and usually considered to have begun with Phineas P. Quimby.
In a fascinating article in *New Thought* magazine, Quimby wrote
about his work in 1837. After experimenting with mesmerism for a
period of years, he concluded that it was not the hypnotism itself,
but the conditioning of the subconscious, which led to the result-
ing changes. Although Quimby had very little formal education,
he had a brilliant, investigative mind and was an original thinker.
In addition, he was a prolific writer and diarist. Records have been
published detailing the development of his findings. He eventually
became a wonderful student of the Bible and duplicated two-thirds
of the Old and New Testament healings. He found that there was
much confusion about the true meaning of many biblical passages,
which caused a misunderstanding and misinterpretation of Jesus
Christ.

All through the 20th century, so many inspired teachers,
authors, ministers, and lecturers contributed to the New Thought

movement. Dr. Charles E. Braden, of the University of Chicago, called these people "spirits in rebellion" because these men and women were truly breaking free from existing dogmatism, rituals, and creeds. (Rebelling at inconsistencies in the old traditions led some individuals to fear religion.) Dr. Braden became discontent with the status quo and refused to conform any longer.

New Thought is an individual practice of the truths of life—a gradual, continuing process. We can learn a bit today, and even more tomorrow. Never will we experience a point where there is nothing more to be discovered. It is infinite, boundless, and eternal. We have all the time we need—eternity. Many of us are impatient with ourselves, and with what we consider our failures. Looking back, though, we discover that these have been periods of learning, and we needn't make these mistakes again. Progress may seem ever so slow: "In patience, possess ye your soul."

In Dr. Murphy's book *Pray Your Way Through It: The Revelation,* he commented that heaven was noted as being "awareness," and Earth, "manifestation." Your new heaven is your revised point of view—your new dimension of consciousness. When we see—that is, see spiritually, we then realize that in the absolute, all is blessed, harmony, boundless love, wisdom, complete peace, and perfection. Identify with these truths, calm the sea of fear; have confidence and faith, and become stronger and surer.

In the books in this series, Dr. Murphy has synthesized the profundities of this power and has put them into an easily under-stood and pragmatic form so that you can apply them immediately to your life. As Dr. Murphy was a Protestant minister, many of his examples and citations come from the Bible. The concepts these passages illustrate should not be viewed as sectarian. Indeed, their messages are universal and are preached in most religions and phi-losophies. He often reiterated that the essence of knowledge is in the law of life and belief. It is not Catholic, Protestant, Muslim, or Hindu; it is pure and simple faith: "Do unto others accordingly."

Dr. Murphy's wife, Dr. Jean Murphy, continued his ministry after his death in 1981. In a lecture she gave in 1986, quoting her late husband, she reiterated his philosophy:

> I want to teach men and women of their Divine Origin, and the powers regnant within them. I want to inform them that this power is within and that they are their own saviors and capable of achieving their own salvation. This is the message of the Bible, and nine-tenths of our confusion today is due to wrongful, literal interpretation of the life-transforming truths offered in it.
>
> I want to reach the majority, the man on the street, the woman overburdened with duty and suppression of her talents and abilities. I want to help others at every stage or level of consciousness to learn of the wonders within.

She said of her husband: "He was a practical mystic, possessed by the intellect of a scholar, the mind of a successful executive, the heart of the poet." His message summed up was: "You are the king, the ruler of your world, for you are one with God."

Joseph Murphy was a firm believer that it was God's plan for people to be healthy, prosperous, and happy. He countered those theologians and others who claimed that desire is evil and urged people to crush it. He said that extinction of our longings means apathy—no feeling, no action. He preached that desire is a gift of God. It is healthy and wholesome to want to become more and better than we were yesterday . . . in the areas of health, abundance, companionship, security, and more. How could these be wrong?

Desire is behind all progress. Without it, nothing would be accomplished. It is the creative power and must be channeled constructively. For example, if one is poor, yearning for wealth wells up from within; if one is ill, there is a wish for health; if lonely, there is a desire for companionship and love.

We must believe that we can improve our lives. A belief—whether it is true, false, or merely indifferent—sustained over a period of time becomes assimilated and is incorporated into our mentality. Unless countermanded by faith of an opposite nature, sooner or later it takes form and is expressed or experienced as fact, form, condition, circumstance, and the events of life. We have the power within us to change negative beliefs to positive ones, and thereby change ourselves for the better.

You give the command and your subconscious mind will faithfully obey it. You will get a reaction or response according to the nature of the thought you hold in your conscious mind. Psychologists and psychiatrists point out that when thoughts are conveyed to your subconscious mind, impressions are made in your brain cells. As soon as this part of you accepts any idea, it proceeds to put it into effect immediately. It works by association of ideas and uses every bit of knowledge that you have gathered in your lifetime to bring about its purpose. It draws on the infinite power, energy, and wisdom within you, lining up all the laws of nature to get its way. Sometimes it seems to bring about an immediate solution to your difficulties, but at other times it may take days, weeks, or longer.

The habitual thinking of your conscious mind establishes deep grooves in your subconscious mind. This is very favorable for you if your recurring thoughts are harmonious, peaceful, and constructive. On the other hand, if you have indulged in fear, worry, and other destructive concepts, the remedy is to recognize the omnipotence of your subconscious and decree freedom, happiness, perfect health, and prosperity. Your subconscious mind, being creative and one with your Divine source, will proceed to create the freedom and happiness that you have earnestly declared.

Now for the first time, Dr. Murphy's lectures have been combined, edited, and updated in six new books that bring his teachings into the 21st century. To enhance and augment this original text, we have incorporated material from some of Jean Murphy's lectures and have added examples of people whose success reflects Dr. Murphy's philosophy.

The other works in this series are listed on the second page of this book, but just reading them will not improve your state of being. To truly maximize your potential, you must study these principles, take them to heart, integrate them into your mentality, and apply them as an integral part of your approach to every aspect of your life.

— **Arthur R. Pell, Ph.D.**, editor

Preface

A happy, successful life flows from a well-balanced mind . . . from someone who has a sense of absolute security and faith in the Great Creator. A sense of uncertainty or uneasiness, on the other hand, dooms us to unhappiness. We must be rooted in the truth of being and feel an unwavering confidence that we're a part of the Divine Intelligence that creates and governs all things. We experience a wonderful sense of peace when we know that nothing can wrench us out of our orbit and that no accident on land or sea—and no disease or discord—can break our union with God.

When we know that nothing can cheat us out of our birthright, every right step must lead to ultimate triumph, and every act of goodness is rewarded, we can serenely reach our highest potential. The belief that a Higher Power has created us and guides us is essential to a well-balanced existence. Once we accept and truly believe this, we lead a God-inspired life.

Can you be a spiritual person without being religious? For centuries, spirituality has been closely allied to religion. People found a spiritual life by attending religious services; observing rituals; and praying in churches, mosques, synagogues, and other places of worship.

This has changed, however, and continues to evolve in the 21st century. More people than ever before are finding spirituality outside of traditional religions. A *Newsday*/**beliefnet.com** poll conducted in the summer of 2005 found that while 79 percent of

Americans described themselves as "spiritual," only 64 percent said that they were "religious."

We can define *spirituality* as the impulse to seek communion with the Divine. It's not necessary to be a member of any organized religion to be spiritual. As long as you believe in a Higher Power and seek inspiration and guidance from God, you're spiritual.

Dr. Joseph Murphy was a firm believer in the spirituality of humankind. As minister-director of the Church of Divine Science, he didn't demand that the congregants follow rigid dogma, but instead encouraged people to seek God in their own way. As a Christian-based religion, Divine Science draws on the Bible for inspiration and guidance but doesn't limit its teachings to biblical texts; it also incorporates insight from many other sources.

Dr. Murphy preaches that every person is inspired by God. The feeling that nothing can separate us from the Divine Power that made and sustains the universe gives us a sense of security and peace. When we awaken in the morning refreshed and rejuvenated, we feel that we've been in touch with the Infinite Intelligence that created us. When we're weary or sad, we long to get back into God's presence and quench our thirst at the great fountainhead of life. That's true spirituality.

Dr. Murphy wants us to realize that we can no longer think of the Divine as our forefathers did—as the stern, remote, and punishing God of the past. We have a new conception of the Eternal One that brings Him down out of the clouds into our everyday life.

We know today that there's no far-off, absentee God but that He's in every atom in the universe. We know that a molecule of matter without God in it is unimaginable because Infinite Intelligence is the reality and soul of every created thing. All beauty and truth and every manifestation of kindness, love, and good is an expression of Him.

God is now so apparent to many of us that nothing else in the world seems half as real as His Presence. We know that we're a vital part of the Divine and that we live, move, and have our being in

Him. We've learned to find God everywhere and in everything. We see Him in every creature and in all "material" things. We know that we take in the Divine Presence with every breath, for It's the great energizing force of the universe.

The new idea of God shows us that He could no more be separated from His creations than the sunbeams could be uncoupled from the sun. Creation is a never-ending process, and we couldn't live for an instant nor take a single breath without the ever-creative principle that is God. We know that whether we're awake or asleep, our hearts beat because of the Great Power that made everything and sustains all life. That's true spirituality.

The time will come when the divisions of religion will fall away and we'll be united as one big family, knowing that we're all children of the one great Father-Mother God. We're entering a higher state of consciousness, becoming aware of the larger truth and a better way of thinking and living born of our new conception of God.

As Dr. Murphy repeats so often in his writings: "If God is for me, who can be against me? One with God is a majority."

— **Arthur R. Pell, Ph.D.,** editor

Chapter One

---•◦•---

The Secret of "I AM That I AM"

*I*n Exodus, we read the story of Moses, who saw God appear
in a burning bush. God said to Moses, "Come now, therefore,
and I will send you to Pharaoh that you may bring My people, the
children of Israel, out of Egypt."

But Moses said to God, "Who am I that I should go to Pha-
raoh, and that I should bring the children of Israel out of Egypt?
. . . Indeed, when I come to the children of Israel and say to them,
'The God of your fathers has sent me to you,' and they say to me,
'What is His Name?' what shall I say to them?"

God answered, "I AM THAT I AM . . . thus you shall say to the
children of Israel, 'I AM has sent me to you . . . The Lord God of
your fathers, the God of Abraham, the God of Isaac, and the God
of Jacob, has sent me to you. This is My name forever, and this is
My memorial to all generations.'"

I am means awareness, being, and Life Principle. The Hindus
use the word *om*, which indicates the same thing. It's the Holy
One Who inhabits Eternity. When you say *I am*, you're announcing the Presence of the Living God within you. You're declaring
yourself to be. The word *that* indicates that which you want to be.
The second *I am* means the answered prayer or the fulfillment of
your desire. You shouldn't repeat "I am that I am" like a parrot, but
thoughtfully state and *feel* what you long to be. Become absorbed

in your dream, and it will begin to gel in your mind. Whatever is impressed on the subconscious is expressed on the screen of space. Then comes the cry of victory and the perfection of the thing you wanted to be.

Whatever you attach to the words *I am* and "emotionalize," you'll become. For instance, if you're looking for your purpose in life, here's a simple prayer that works wonderfully. I've taught it to many people throughout the world. Say to yourself: "I am in my true place. I am doing what I love to do. I am divinely happy and prospered." Say that feelingly and meaningfully. Then the deeper mind will take over and open up all doors for you. Your hidden talents will be revealed to you and you'll find yourself in your true place, meaning that you'll be expressing yourself at your highest possible level.

Take your attention away from your problem, whether it's sickness, lack, or limitation. Focus on your ideal and claim yourself to be what you long to be. You can say, for example, "I am whole, perfect, vital, and strong." Rejoice and feel it. Then the old conditions will pass away, and you'll experience the joy of the answered prayer.

The Bible says: "The Lord will fight for you, and you shall hold your peace." You're saved from fear, superstition, disease, lack, and limitations of all kinds because you're aware of the God Presence within and your capacity to contact Him. *When you call upon Him, He answers you. He will be with you in trouble; He will set you on high because you have known His name.*

⌑✦⌑

In Revelations, it's written: "Behold, I stand at the door, and knock: if any man hear my voice, and open the door, I will come in to him, and will sup with him, and he with me."

The God Presence is always knocking at the door of your heart. It's forever seeking to express Itself at higher levels through you.

You're a channel of the Divine; therefore, you must listen to the murmurings and whisperings of your soul because God is telling you, "Come up higher; I need you to play a greater role." Your desires are a gift from God.

Then call upon the Infinite Intelligence that always responds to you. If you ask for a fish, It won't give you a serpent; and if you request bread, it won't give you a stone because It always responds by providing exactly what you ask for. If you were lost in the woods, Divine guidance or God's light would illuminate your path and reveal the way out to you. The answer is always inside you because God dwells within.

Have a deep conviction that all is well even when conditions seem negative. Live in the atmosphere of victory, and victory will be yours. Having seen the end, you've willed the means to the realization of your goal. Contemplate the happy result and realize that all of the power of the godhead will flow to that focal point of attention. *I am* is Creative Force.

⊨✢⊨

Be careful not to create negative results by saying things such as "I am dumb," I am inferior," "I am lonely," "I am no good," "I am sick," and so on. Remember that whatever you attach to *I am* with emotion and feeling, you become. All these things will come to pass as you continue to reiterate them because they sink into your subconscious and—just like seeds—grow after their kind. Therefore, be sure that you don't make any statements about yourself that you don't want to be true.

⊨✢⊨

The ancient Hebrews said that in order to create, God divided Himself into two—the male and the female. Then God conceived Himself to be the sun, the moon, and the stars. He pictured Himself as human and brought forth all the things in this universe. Everything was created this way, including you. You're male and female, too. Your conscious mind is the male; your subconscious is the female. Whatever you impress upon the subconscious, the mind brings it forth, whether it's good or bad.

※✛※

You may say, "I'm a man," "I'm a woman," "I'm an American, "I'm a doctor," I'm a Republican," or I'm a Democrat." These are facts about you, but they're limitations of the Infinite One, for God is unbounded. As the philosopher Spinoza said, "To define God is to deny Him."

You're an individualized expression of God Consciousness. Whitman wrote that man is a "god walking the earth." In other words, every person is an aspect of the Divine. You were born with certain talents and abilities, and you're unique. There's no one in the entire world like you because you're *you*. Perhaps you're mechanically inclined, musically gifted, or have other aptitudes. Just as no two snowflakes or leaves are alike, no two human beings are the same. We're all equal in the eyes of God; but we're not equal in strength, wisdom, understanding, or anything else.

※✛※

Seek ye first the kingdom of God and His righteousness, and all things shall be added unto you. What does this biblical statement mean? It's saying that the kingdom of God—your consciousness or mind—is within you. Your state of consciousness is what you think, believe, and imagine yourself to be. All these things are then dramatized on the screen of space.

You must first go within and claim what you want to be. Then the Divine Spirit inside you will honor and fulfill your desire. Become quiet, shut the doors of your senses, and pray to your Father, Who is the Life Principle and the Source of all things.

━┿━

In the beginning was the Word, and the Word was with God, and the Word was God. The *word* is thought expressed. We're told that the word was God because it's creative. For example, if you hypnotize a woman and put your finger on her neck and say, "This is a red-hot poker," she'll get a blister. The thought and the manifestation are one. This happens because thoughts are things. What you feel, you attract; and what you imagine, you become. You can use this great law to attain what you desire instead of to create pain.

━┿━

Your concept of yourself determines your future, and your world reflects your thoughts. After all, isn't it natural for an apple seed to become an apple tree? Seeds always grow after their kind. If you're full of hatred, resentment, and hostility, you certainly can't express love, peace, beauty, or joy. These negative emotions get snarled up in the subconscious and must come forth as unpleasant results, for the law of mind is always perfect. It constantly brings forth the likeness of our conception of ourselves.

━┿━

Everything you see comes out of the Absolute, for there's only One Presence. It's eternal, whole, and perfect. It's the silent, ruling Being dwelling in the hearts of all people. Every single thing you see is God made manifest. It's the Divine appearing as the sun, the moon, the stars, the trees, the mud, and the rivers. As it says in the Upanishads, God thinks, and worlds appear.

The Holy Grail that people have been looking for down through the ages is actually something that passes through your lips a thousand times a day: *I am.* The *I am* is the Living Spirit within you. It was never born and will never die. Water wets it not, fire burns it not, and wind blows it not away. That's a wonderful thing to know.

⊯✝⊱

Stop condemning yourself. Realize that you can now claim what you want to be, what you long to possess, and what you yearn to do. Your affirmation will gradually sink down into your subconscious, becoming a conviction. Then your limitations will disintegrate, and you'll rise like a phoenix from the ashes of the old and become a new person.

You must subdue your thoughts of poverty and resurrect the belief in God's opulence. Believe that it's God's will for you to be joyous, free, vital, and strong. Claim that the wholeness of God is flowing through you and remove your attention from the multitude of reasons why you can't achieve something. Focus on your ideal—nourish and sustain it—and the answer will come. Keep on keeping on, and the day will break and all shadows will flee.

⊯✝⊱

You can't contact the God Presence within you if you're full of self-pity and condemnation. When you pray, you must be filled with compassion. This love is an outreaching of the heart and an emanation of goodwill. It's wishing for all people what you desire for yourself. Forgive the people who have hurt you and pray that they'll enjoy love, peace, harmony, joy, and all the blessings of life. You'll know that you've forgiven when you can think of them and feel no sting.

If you hear that something marvelous has happened to someone who cheated or undermined you and you feel resentful, this means that the roots of hatred are still in your conscious mind wreaking havoc. The healing power of God won't move through a contaminated consciousness any more than water flows through a sink when the pipe is corroded or full of debris. However, the healing water is always there waiting to flow when the blockages are removed.

⊨✠⊨

You need to put God first in your life. Do you say, "I'm too busy"? Then you're claiming that you don't have time for the Infinite Presence. This is wrong because you shouldn't give power to any created thing—not to circumstances, people, the stars, the sun, or the moon. The thinker is greater than his thought, the artist is greater than his art, and the Creator is greater than His creation. Therefore, scientific people don't give power to any created thing in this universe. On the contrary, they give their allegiance, devotion, and loyalty to the *I am* within, which is the only Presence, Cause, and Substance.

The minute you give power to anything besides God, you're practicing idolatry. In other words, you're living with evil in your own mind. Remember the great command: "Thou shalt have no other gods before me." Put God *first* in your life, and then everything will unfold wonderfully. If you're experiencing lots of chaos, confusion, or scarcity, it's because you're putting something before God.

Before you go to work in the morning, sit quietly and ask for Divine guidance and right action. Claim peace and harmony, and the love of God will flood your mind, your heart, and your entire being.

⊨✠⊨

When some engineers or scientists have a so-called insurmountable difficulty, they say, "God sent me here to solve this problem. This challenge is Divinely outmatched because Infinite Intelligence knows only the answer." They realize that the light of God shines in them and reveals the solution. They know in their heart that the Power of the godhead always responds.

There's only One Power and Presence. It's an ancient truth. It's called the *burning bush* in the Bible because It's the everlasting light that was never born and will never die. It's the Divine Presence within you. *I am* has no beginning or end and is fixed in the hearts of all people.

Remember that God is your true nature and that no person, place, condition, or circumstance can thwart your good. There's no power in the entire world that can prevent the flow of the Spirit through you. It's Almighty Presence, and that's your real identity.

⌖

You must be alert and take advantage of the opportunities all around you. You shouldn't expect to be rewarded for indolence, apathy, or laziness. As Emerson wrote: "Shallow men believe in luck, believe in circumstances. It was somebody's name, or he happened to be there at the time, or, it was so then, and another day it would have been otherwise. Strong men believe in cause and effect."

Never say, "I can't," "I'm too weak," or "There's no way out." When you do, you're shortening your life, and your cells become more sensitive to pain. Instead, affirm: "God loves and cares for me. Divine compassion surrounds and enfolds me. I lead a charmed life. Infinite love goes before me, making my way straight and perfect." When you do that, marvelous things will happen. If there's discord at the office or in your home—or if you have an emotional problem or are suffering from an illness—say, "God is here and will show me the way. Divine Spirit heals me now." Then the road will open up, and you'll surmount all difficulties.

⌖

You become what you think about all day long, and your character is the totality of your thoughts and beliefs. In order to experience good fortune, realize that you're the master of your thoughts, emotions, and reactions in life. You're the maker and shaper of your conditions, experiences, and events. Every thought that you accept in your conscious mind takes root in your subconscious and eventually blossoms. Positive thoughts bring forth good fruit, while negative thoughts create a rotten harvest.

⁂

Fall in love with a higher image of yourself. When any fear comes into your mind, say: "I exalt God in the midst of me." There's no fear in God, for He's the Only Power. He's the All-Wise, Eternal One Who lives in all of our hearts. Affirm: "I am whole, illumined, and inspired. I am a child of God and am joyous, free, healthy, and perfect." You can sing these words, and they'll enter your subconscious and manifest in your life. Whatever is impressed on the subconscious manifests itself, whether it's good, bad, or indifferent. Do you say, "I'm weak and bad"? Don't do it! Instead, affirm: "I am a child of the Living God; I am heir to all that is."

⁂

Angry people are at war with themselves. They fight with everybody because they're battling with themselves. As within, so without. If you don't have love and harmony in your own heart, there won't be peace in your external world. *Great peace have they who love thy law, and nothing shall offend them. Thou wilt keep him in perfect peace whose mind is stayed on thee.*

Focus your mind on God and the river of peace will flow through you. If you keep your attention centered on Divine love and beauty, then your path will be pleasant and harmonious.

⁂

William K. had a severe angina attack. The doctor told him that his heart condition was incurable and that he had only three or four months to live, but William refused to accept this diagnosis.

He said, "I must live." He told me that he remembered the law of mind and began to sing to himself in bed all day long, saying: "I am whole, perfect, and strong; I am healed, vital, and joyous." He began to affirm these things morning, noon, and night and even found himself waking up in the wee hours repeating his claims.

He was completely healed in two weeks' time, and the cardiogram showed that his heart was normal. William's story illustrates that whatever you attach to the words *I am* with conviction, you become. God is the only Healing Presence and is available to everyone. He's there to help in times of trouble. Remember the great truth that God always answers when you call upon Him.

⊰✛⊱

I used to lecture near the Himalayas. One of the yogis there told me that often he would go into the jungle; but the snakes, tigers, and other wild animals would never harm him. In fact, he said that sometimes he would use a tiger as a pillow. Why wasn't the yogi attacked? Because he saw the Presence of God in all His creatures and was at peace with them. That's absolutely true.

Similarly, many trappers and hunters will tell you that if you look at a bear and are at peace, you'll radiate love and understanding to that animal, and he won't attack you. If you run away, however, you'll be mauled.

⊰✛⊱

Begin with the end in mind. If you start your marriage with love, faith, and confidence, you'll experience those things. The thought in the mind and its manifestation are one. For example, a man in Detroit told me that he started a restaurant on a shoestring. He affirmed to himself: "I am succeeding in doing the right thing and practicing the golden rule. I am a tremendous success." People backed him and loaned him money, and he has a thriving business today. Why? Because he began with faith and confidence.

Begin the day with joyous expectancy, and blessings will unfold in your life. Your attitude will bring you success. However, if you start out filled with fear and anxiety, you'll create failure. Therefore, begin every morning with prayer and thoughts of your good, and Divine love and light will illuminate your path now and forevermore.

In a Nutshell

When you say *I am*, you're announcing the Presence of the Living God within you. Whatever you attach to *I am* with feeling and understanding, you become.

Take your attention away from your problem, whether it's sickness, lack, or limitation. Instead, focus on your ideal, goal, or objective. Claim yourself to be what you long to be. Rejoice and feel it. Then the old condition will pass away, and you'll experience the joy of an answered prayer.

Have a deep conviction that all is well in spite of evidence to the contrary. Live in the mental atmosphere of victory, and victory will be yours.

The kingdom of God is within you. It's your consciousness or what you think, believe, and feel—the invisible part of you. It's what you imagine yourself to be.

People down through the ages have sought the Holy Grail, and all this time it has passed through their lips a thousand times a day. It's the *I am*, which announces the Living Spirit within you. It was never born and will never die; water wets it not, and fire burns it not. That's a wonderful thing to realize.

Stop condemning yourself. Realize that you can now claim what you want to be, possess, and do. Your desire will gradually sink into your subconscious and become a conviction as you nourish and sustain it. Then your limitations will disintegrate, and you'll rise like a phoenix from the ashes of the old and become a new person.

The reason you experience so much chaos and confusion is because you're putting something before God. Put God first, and then everything will go right in your life. Before you go to work in the morning, sit down and ask for Divine guidance and right action. Claim peace and harmony, and the love of God will flood your mind, heart, and entire being.

Never say, "I can't," "I'm too weak," or "There's no way out." If you're experiencing discord or illness, affirm: "God is here and can show me the way. Infinite Intelligence heals me now." Then the road will open up, and you'll surmount all difficulties.

In order to experience good fortune, realize that you're the master of your thoughts, emotions, and reactions in life. Every thought that you accept in your conscious mind and "emotional-ize" takes root in your subconscious and eventually blossoms. Positive thoughts bring forth good fruit, while negative thoughts create a rotten harvest. Begin the day with love, faith, and confidence, and you'll experience these qualities in your life.

Chapter Two

The Great Secret of the Ages

*M*any people in this world believe in black magic, voodoo, or "the evil eye." They think that outside influences can make them miserable. Such beliefs are false, yet those who hold them actually cause themselves to become sick and even die.

The truth is that other people's suggestions have no power unless you give them power. It's your own thought that creates everything in your life. You have the ability to completely reject any negative suggestions and unite mentally with the Omnipotence within you. Then you're in tune with the Infinite.

To lead a truly full and happy life, you must awaken to the great secret of the ages, which is expressed in Deuteronomy 6:4: "Hear, 0 Israel: The Lord our God, the Lord is one." There's only One Presence and Power—not two, three, or a thousand. The greatest of all truths is that Divine Spirit moves as harmony, beauty, and love in you.

⌖

Many churches teach young children, who are highly impressionable, about a punitive God and a devil who's determined to tempt them. They're warned that if they're very bad, they might go to hell and suffer forever. These kids envision God up in the heavens on a golden throne surrounded by angels, and the devil down below in the flames of perdition.

Teaching children these fallacies creates a psychology of fear and doom that can destroy their lives. The fact is that heaven and hell exist only in our minds. There's no devil with hooves and a pointed tail—that's a figment of a twisted imagination. We each create our own paradise and suffering through the way we think, imagine, feel, and believe.

⊭✝⊭

In ancient times, primitive people believed that gods created all pleasure and that evil spirits were responsible for all pain and misery. When a flood or earthquake occurred, they didn't understand the geological causes and attributed the disaster to the wrath of the deities. Then they proceeded to offer up sacrifices to appease them.

A belief in two powers—good and evil—is a holdover of these old, superstitious ideas. In fact, the forces of nature are neutral. The same wind can cast a boat onto the rocks or carry it safely to the harbor. You can use electrical energy to run a motor or to electrocute someone. Water can quench your thirst or become a tsunami and drown thousands of people.

In short, good and evil aren't part of nature; they're in the mind of the individual. If you think positive thoughts, blessings follow; and if you think negative thoughts, unpleasant results manifest. The basic truth is that your own essence is Divine and your thoughts are therefore creative. When your thoughts are God's thoughts, His power is behind your desire for good. It's the only force in the world.

⊭✝⊭

Lisa L. came to see me because she was greatly distressed. She told me that some people in her former church were praying against her because she'd left their group, and now everything was going wrong in her life. She believed that she was cursed and that something very bad was going to happen. The truth is that these people had no power. I explained to her that the "curse" was really her own negative use of the law of the subconscious mind. Her fearful thoughts were manifesting in painful conditions.

The suggestions of others had become part of Lisa's own subconscious, and since her thoughts were creative, she was hurting herself. She didn't realize that she was transferring the power within herself to members of her former church, not knowing that they actually had no influence at all. I explained to her that she should immediately cease giving others control over her life.

All she had to do was align herself with the Infinite within her and give It her devotion and loyalty. Then nothing harmful would happen to her. She began to affirm: "I dwell in the secret place of the Most High, and I abide under the shadow of the Almighty. I will say of the Lord, 'He is my refuge and my fortress. My God, in Him will I trust.'" This prayer comes from Psalm 91.

I told Lisa, "Look at those people as extremely ignorant and have compassion for them. The real and ultimate power is God, Who moves as harmony, beauty, love, and peace. Remember that a suggestion has no power unless you *give* it power. Consciously unite with the Infinite Presence within you and constantly realize that the spell of God's love surrounds and enfolds you. Affirm that you lead a charmed life. Whenever you think of the church people, immediately affirm: 'I release you to God and let you go.'"

As she practiced the above simple truths, she was at peace and actually laughed at herself for having given power to the suggestions of others. After about a week, she heard that five of these women had become extremely ill and that one had passed on. She was no longer receiving their evil thoughts, and their negativity had boomeranged with double force upon themselves.

Lisa's story illustrates that when what you greatly fear has come upon you, you need to reverse your thoughts. And conversely, when wonderful experiences come to you, embrace them. This is the great eternal truth of God.

❈✛❈

In my book *Telepsychics: The Magic Power of Perfect Living,* I reported the story of a woman in Honolulu who had married outside of her race and religion. Since her father was a kahuna (a native priest) and had "magical powers," he was determined to use sorcery to break up her marriage. This woman was a university graduate and had majored in psychology, yet she lived in fear of her father's curse. I explained to her that if love united her and her husband, no person or condition could break up her marriage. God is love, and when two hearts beat as one, all the excommunications and curses in the world are like using a peashooter to fire at a great battleship.

This explanation greatly relieved her. She said to her father, "Dad, I'm no longer afraid of you. You're to be pitied. You think that you have power, but you're just using negative suggestions, and that which you suggest or wish for another, you create in your own experience. The power is within *me,* and I know my oneness with God. His love surrounds me and watches over me. Whenever I think of you, I affirm: 'God is for me, so no one can be against me. I am free.'"

She blessed her father and released him. Shortly afterward, she contacted me, saying that her father continued to hate her and her husband and had written to her that his sorcery would destroy both of them. However, she paid no attention to his threats, and a few weeks later he dropped dead on the street. She said that her dad had killed himself with hatred, and she was right. Hatred, jealousy, and hostility are a denial of the Divine Presence within and kill love, peace, and joy. All of her father's destructive thoughts recoiled on himself, and the double blow proved too much for him. Remember that whatever you wish upon another, you create and manifest in your own body and experience.

❈✛❈

In ancient Egyptian times, the multitudes believed that their priests had the power to curse those who displeased or irritated them. The religious rulers of that day took advantage of the ignorance of the people. However, Moses saw through the chicanery, deceit, and trickery of the Egyptian priests; and they were completely dumbfounded by him. They were afraid of him and agreed to let him and his entire following leave the camp where they'd been detained. Moses taught the oneness of Divine Spirit. He proclaimed, "We're all children of the *I am*." His awareness scattered the Egyptians' negative ideas to the winds.

It's absolutely necessary that you understand that harmony, beauty, love, peace, joy, and all the blessings of life come from the Holy Source. There's only *One* Power. God can't do anything unloving or wish pain for you because He's boundless love, harmony, and bliss.

⊶✛⊷

God is eternal life and never dies. You're only dead when you don't know that God walks and talks in you and that thoughts are things. If you don't realize that you attract what you think about, then you're dead to the truth of being.

Turn to the Living Spirit Almighty within, open your mind and heart, and affirm daily: "God *is*, and His Presence flows through me as harmony, beauty, love, peace, joy, and abundance. Divine Intelligence watches over me, and I am always surrounded by the sacred circle of God's eternal love."

When you recognize the supremacy of the Spirit and the power of your own thoughts, you'll find that all your ways are peaceful and pleasant. It's wonderful to know that God is the Only Presence and Power. So stop going through life mechanically, repeating the same old clichés, thinking the same tired thoughts, and reacting in an automatic way. When your car becomes old and worn out, you get a new one. In the same way, it's essential to acquire a new image of yourself and a transformed awareness of life. Expect the best and anticipate a most glorious future. Believe that it's possible and you'll experience the joy and thrill of the fulfillment of your dream. Cease going around in circles, keep your eyes on God's glory, and move forward in the light.

⇥✚⇤

What is the level of your perception? There are many things that exist that you're not aware of. For example, radio waves are flowing through the atmosphere even though you can't see them. Are you conscious of the Divinity within that can heal and inspire you, reveal your hidden talents, and work miracles in your life? This untapped Power is *always* there, and you can begin to use It now.

To illustrate, Dr. Lothar von Blankschmid, an aerospace scientist, told me that whenever he has a problem in his work in the engineering department at Lockheed, he stills the wheels of his mind and quietly affirms: "Infinite Intelligence within me casts light on this project." Suddenly his mind is illuminated with the answer, which sometimes appears as a graph. The God Presence within him always responds to his requests.

⇥✚⇤

If you want to go to San Francisco, you obviously must leave the place where you currently are. Similarly, if you want to be joyous, successful, and prosperous, you must leave behind old grudges, negativity, and self-condemnation. You need to develop a new self-image. Picture yourself as who you want to be. Be faithful to the new image, and it will sink into your subconscious mind, where it will gestate in the darkness and come forth in your experience as the joy of an answered prayer. You'll become renewed in God and go from glory to glory.

Direct your mind joyously, positively, and definitely in the direction of advancement, promotion, and accomplishment. As you dwell on your new image of yourself and sense the reality of it, your mind will cause your idea to gel within you and become a living fact.

Don't go to work or drive home the same way every day, and don't read the same newspapers all the time—try allowing new information to enter your life. Stop talking the same old way and avoid using clichés in your speech. Meet people and make new friends, and you may perceive opportunities and values that you never saw before. Think about everything and everyone from the standpoint of the One Power and you'll achieve wonderful things.

⊯✦⊱

Make it a habit to meditate on the wonders of the Infinite and marvelous events will unfold in your life. Realize that God is guiding you and Divine right action governs your life. God is love, and His compassion fills your soul now. His peace imbues your mind and body, and His wholeness and beauty flow through you. In Him, there's fullness of joy and no darkness at all. You're a clear channel for the Divine, and if you think and feel these truths, you'll experience all of the blessings of life.

God is waiting for you. He says, "Call upon me, and I will answer you. I'll be with you in your time of trouble. I will set you on High because you have known my name." He also states, "Before you call, I will answer; and while you are yet speaking, I will hear." Before you ask, the solution is already there, for the Infinite knows *only* the answers.

⊯✦⊱

Horace L. had gone bankrupt a short time before he came to consult with me. He'd developed ulcers and high blood pressure. He was, as he said, a "mess." He believed that he was cursed and that God was punishing him for his past sins. These were all false beliefs.

I explained to him that as long as he believed that God was out to get him, he'd suffer for the simple reason that all beliefs take form as experiences, conditions, and events. I gave him the following prayer, which worked miracles in his life. It will do the same for you as you read it now. Let it sink into your mind and soul:

> *There is but One Presence and Power. This Power is within me as mind and spirit. It moves through me as harmony, health, and peace. I think, speak, and act from the standpoint of Infinite Intelligence. I know that thoughts are things. What I feel, I attract; and what I imagine, I become. I constantly dwell on these truths. Divine law and order reign supreme and operate in all phases of my life. Divine success and prosperity are mine now. Eternal love fills my soul, and Infinite wisdom governs all my transactions. Whenever fear or worry come into my mind, I affirm immediately: "God is guiding me now" or "God knows the answer." I make a habit of this, and I know that miracles are happening in my life.*

Horace prayed out loud in this manner five or six times daily, and at the end of a month, his health was restored and he was made a partner in a growing business. His entire life was transformed. The new idea enthroned in his mind compelled him to express the riches of life and become successful, for the laws of the subconscious mind are compulsive. Yes, remember that ideas are our masters—they control and govern us. If you plant in your mind the kinds of ideas and suggestions that Horace used, wonders will begin to occur in *your* life.

⊯✛⊯

I talked with Dianne M., who was being treated for arthritis. She'd been praying, but she said, "Every time I begin to think of health, harmony, and peace, thoughts of hopelessness, pain, and deformity fill my mind and push out my thoughts of well-being." The reason for this was that since infancy, she'd been conditioned to believe that some diseases, including arthritis, are incurable. She seemed to lack the capacity to decisively choose perfect health.

She was able to neutralize this attitude, however, after she followed my instructions. I explained to her that the first thing she had to do was rid her mind of the belief in two powers—one that causes sickness and one that's responsible for health. She actually failed to perceive the simple truth that the cause of all sickness, poverty, and misery in the world is the prevalent belief in good and evil. When you believe in this duality, you can't ask God for anything and you're tossed about by the winds of fear.

Dianne decided to transform her mental focus and began to affirm boldly:

> *I believe once and for all that there is but One Supreme Power, which is all wholeness, beauty, and perfection. I know that the greatest secret in life is to believe in the One Power, which is Infinitely good. I consciously claim that the healing love of the Divine Spirit that created me is now dissolving all of the deposits and disease in my body, which do not belong there. I am a temple of the Living God, and I glorify Him in my body.*

As Dianne continued to repeat this prayer, her faith in the One Presence increased, and her belief in an evil power gradually diminished until her conviction that there's only One Power reigned supreme in her mind. She continued with therapy, and gradually her limbs became supple. All the calcareous deposits disappeared, the edema subsided, and her body became a channel for the Infinite Intelligence, which always moves as beauty, love, and peace.

※✦※

A woman once told me about her wonderful philosophy of life. She'd even written a thesis entitled "The Way of Life," which was scientifically and spiritually sound. However, her personal life was chaotic. She was only 25 but had been divorced four times. She was an alcoholic and was unable to pay her rent.

I explained to her that although her philosophy was solid, it was meaningless if she didn't apply it in her life. In other words, her head knowledge had to become *heart* knowledge. She needed to assimilate these truths until they became a living part of her in the same way that a piece of bread becomes a part of the bloodstream.

You know, you can score 100 percent on a metaphysical examination and still be a failure in life because your knowledge is only intellectual. These truths must be incorporated into your subconscious mind so that you'll be compelled to express them in your life. As the Bible says: "As a man thinketh in his heart [not his head], so is he."

The woman began to regularly affirm: "God is love, and His love fills my soul. God is peace, and His peace fills my mind and body. God is wholeness, beauty, and perfection, and those qualities are mine now. God is joy, and His joy is my joy. I feel wonderful!"

As she systematically saturated her mind and heart with these truths, her life was transformed.

※✦※

A scientist puts forth a theory or a hypothesis, but before it's generally accepted as a scientific fact, it has to be validated objectively; otherwise, it remains merely an unproven theory. In the same way, the truths that you affirm must be made flesh, which means that they must be embodied in your experience. You must demonstrate what you believe. You may have relatives or friends who know nothing about metaphysics but are leading marvelous lives because they have a rugged faith in the goodness of God in the land of the living. They believe in success and health, and although they don't have a theoretical knowledge of the law of mind, they're still putting it to use. You must also apply the great truths and use them in your daily life.

⊰✦⊱

People often ask me, "If God exists, why doesn't He end war, crime, and disease?" You've heard that question, I suppose. It has been asked down through the ages. People cry, "Why does God allow me to suffer so?" "Why did He thrust sickness upon me?" or "I'm so good . . . I follow all the rules of the church, give money to charities, and read holy books, but I'm in pain." The answer is very simple: Infinite Intelligence dwells within all people. Every time you think, you're using this Creative Power for good or for evil. What are *you* thinking about? You do have volition and are responsible for what you believe.

⊰✦⊱

When we were very young, our minds were impressionable. We weren't capable of doing much abstract reasoning. Therefore, we accepted the weird ideas that were suggested by our parents and others. It's just the same as if you hypnotized a person and said to him, "You now see a snake crawling across the room." His subconscious mind would automatically accept that suggestion, and he would see the thought-form of a snake. To him, it would seem real. It's like an eight-year old boy I knew who was somewhat emotionally unstable. He was constantly reading about the Blessed Virgin Mary appearing at Lourdes and Guadalupe. He was always saying to himself, "Someday I'll see the Virgin Mary." He was hypnotizing himself and kept a picture of Mary in his prayer book. One day we were out for a walk and he said, "I see the Virgin Mary!"

"What does she look like?" I asked.

"Well," he said, "she's dressed in white, and she has beads." He was describing exactly the same picture as the one in his prayer book because he'd hypnotized himself. It was a hallucination. I suppose if you had such a hallucination and told everyone about it, you'd have about a million people claiming to see the same thing because the mind can be so impressionable.

⊯✛⊯

There's but One Power that you can use to cast light on any problem. If you say, "I'm all mixed up and confused, and there's no way out," you're claiming that Infinite Intelligence doesn't have the answers. At that moment, you're an atheist. If you believe in God, you know that He's the Infinite Intelligence that creates all things and knows and sees everything.

Many people who profess to be Christians are really atheists. They say, "My daughter is hopeless; she has an incurable disease." They're claiming that God made her from a cell but can't heal her. And according to their belief, it is done unto them. They live in the darkness of confusion created by their own ignorance or misuse of the Supreme Power. They create evil in their experience by thinking negatively and destructively.

However, you can always create peace by dwelling mentally on that which is true, lovely, and noble. Ask yourself this question: How am *I* using the One Power? You can never really grow and expand spiritually until you come to the absolute conviction that there is but One Power.

⌖

Every belief tends to manifest itself. Therefore, if you believe that you have to reincarnate again and again on this earthly plane to atone for your sins, you're definitely placing yourself in the chains of bondage. You can't deny it or circumvent it because whatever you believe in your subconscious comes to pass. Your deeper mind can't take a joke. Therefore, if you have such a limiting belief, you're putting yourself in thralldom and can't grow spiritually. Why would you think along these lines? Frankly, I don't understand it when people talk this way. Heavens! Haven't they ever heard a word of truth? Don't they understand how the mind works?

After all, the first lesson of the mind is: "It is done unto you as you believe." Therefore, if you believe that you must work out your karma, you're imprisoning yourself. The Life Principle doesn't judge or punish you—It can't. You punish *yourself.* If you burn yourself, the Divine Presence forgives you, gives you new skin and tissue, and reduces your pain. If you cut yourself, It heals you. God always seeks to restore you, so direct your vision toward perfect health, harmony, and peace of mind. The Spirit in you is timeless and formless. Why, then, should you think that you have to atone for something or expiate your karma?

⌖

You become what you contemplate, so think big from now on. Enlarge your vision and contemplate freedom, peace of mind, abundance, and goodwill for all. Nothing can oppose you, and there's no reason whatsoever to worry. All successful men and women possess one outstanding characteristic: their ability to make prompt decisions and to persist in carrying these choices through to completion. So make a decision *now* that you want to experience more and more of the Infinite ocean of life and love within you.

※✦※

You can be absolutely certain that the mental picture to which you remain faithful will be developed in your subconscious mind and consequently manifest in your experience. Jesus said: "Today you shall be with me in paradise." He didn't mean tomorrow, next year, or 20 years from now, but *right now.* The minute you turn to the God Presence with faith and adoration in your heart, It turns to you.

Forget the past. It's dead. Nothing matters but this moment. When you change this moment and keep it changed, your whole life is transformed. A new beginning is a new end. That's the simplest of all truths. *I am the Alpha and the Omega, the Beginning and the End, says the Lord.* Therefore, begin with faith and confidence. Make a decision that you want to become a new person in God, and the past will be forgotten.

I'm not talking about perfunctory thought but about the intense desire to change your heart. *Blessed are those who hunger and thirst for righteousness, for they shall be filled.* People who fill their minds with the truths of God clean out a stable that might have been dirty for 40 or 50 years, for there's no time or space in the Eternal Presence.

※✦※

The Bible says: "Perfect love casts out fear . . . but he who fears has not been made perfect in love." Love is the spirit of God. It doesn't have height or depth, and it neither comes nor goes. It's an outreaching of the heart. It's seeing the God Presence in all people everywhere. Experience the God Presence in yourself, your wife, your husband, your children, your friends, and your associates. Call It forth. Say: "I see God in everyone; and God's love, light, truth, and beauty are now resurrected in the mind and heart of these people."

Wonders will unfold in your life as you start to do this. Begin now to practice the presence of God. See Him everywhere—in trees, sermons, stones, songs, running brooks, and every other place. *If I take the wings of morning, and dwell in the uttermost parts of the sea, even there Your hand shall lead me, and Your right hand shall hold me.*

⁻⁺⁻

Millions of people don't know that when they say "I am," they're announcing the Presence and Power of God within themselves. *I am* means being, life, and awareness. It's the Eternal One Who is whole, complete, and perfect. It's the God Presence in you. Honor and exalt It. God is the giver and the gift, and you're the receiver. Everything has already been given; so the only thing that you can give God is glory, honor, faith, and trust.

Turn your eyes to the God Presence and you'll rise higher and higher every day. You'll go from power to power and from glory to glory. God keeps you on this path now.

In a Nutshell

The truth is that your essence is the Lord God Almighty. Your only power is your thought, which is creative. When your thoughts are God's thoughts, God's power backs your desire for good.

It's absolutely necessary that you understand that harmony, beauty, love, peace, joy, and all the blessings of life come from the One Source. God can't do anything unloving because He's boundless love and peace. He can't wish pain or sadness on you, for He's absolute joy.

Acquire a new image of yourself and a new interpretation of life. Expect the best and look forward with anticipation to a most glorious future. Believe it's possible, and you'll experience the joy and thrill of the fulfillment of your dream.

Direct your mind joyously, positively, and definitely in the direction of advancement, promotion, and accomplishment. As you dwell on your dreams in your mind, the ideas will gel and become a living fact.

The thoughts that you affirm must be made flesh, which means they must be embodied in your experience. You must demonstrate your religious beliefs in all areas of your life because faith without works is useless.

You become what you focus on, so think big from now on. Contemplate freedom, peace of mind, abundance, and goodwill for all. There's nothing to oppose you and no reason to worry because you're Divine Spirit.

Chapter Three

What the *Will of God* Really Means

A tragic error that many people throughout the world make is to assume that God's will for them might be sickness, misfortune, or even death. In fact, God is Life with no beginning or end. He therefore can't wish death for us. That's a complete contradiction. How could God or Life die? On the contrary, the tendency of Life is to express Itself as beauty, joy, harmony, love, wisdom, and order through us.

The truth is that the will of the Infinite for you and for everybody is something greater than you could possibly conceive. God wants you to enjoy perfect health, true expression, great prosperity, and marvelous opportunities to serve others. So many individuals don't realize the magnificent truth that the will of the Infinite transcends their fondest dreams. In this scientific age, it's shocking to hear people say that God intends for them to experience destruction and pain.

If you're living in poverty or are ill, lonesome, or frustrated, you can be absolutely certain that you're not expressing the will of God. God's doesn't want anyone to get sick or die. For instance, I remember something that happened in New York many years ago. A clergyman visited a home in which a four-year-old boy had died. The clergyman told the parents that their son's death was God's will. However, a subsequent investigation showed that although the little boy had been suffering from an extremely high fever, the father and the mother had been intoxicated and didn't call the doctor. The death of the toddler was due to negligence, indifference, and drunkenness on the part of the parents. It had nothing to do with the will of God.

═╬═

There is no death. When you pass on to the next dimension, you put on a new body. You have bodies to infinity, and you go from glory to glory forever. Life is an endless unfolding of the Infinite Being that wants to express Itself through you as beauty, love, and harmony. You are not a victim, but an expression of Divine Spirit.

═╬═

If you want to enjoy greater health, create a better home for your family, become more proficient in your profession, have a greater measure of wealth, be more successful, get along better with your neighbors, or sing more beautifully, your wish is aligned with the tendency of Life, which is to benefit humanity. In other words, if your plan will help people in any way, you're operating in conformity with God's will, which is peace, joy, and compassion.

═╬═

All prayers are answered according to the level of your belief. As Matthew 9 says: "According to your faith will it be done to you." This isn't faith in a creed or a dogma but in the creative laws of your own mind. If you say that God's will is for you to experience pain and difficulty, that's your prayer. Of course, you'll suffer accordingly because you're giving the wrong instructions to your subconscious mind.

-≈✝≈-

Alcoholics may talk about giving up drinking. However, that's just wishful thinking and won't work. Their idle hope must become a conviction before they'll be healed. They must speak with authority. They need to realize that they have the power to unite with the Infinite Presence and call upon It, knowing that It will respond. Only then can they claim: "Freedom, peace of mind, and sobriety are mine. There's an Almighty Power backing me up. The doctor is congratulating me on my perfect health."

When they suffer the jitters of withdrawal, they need to repeat the above affirmation to themselves. They know that the Divine Spirit supports them. As they continue to do this, their wish becomes a conviction that takes root in their subconscious—and whatever is impressed in the deeper mind is expressed on the screen of space. That's the power of the Almighty. Their will becomes God's will.

-≈✝≈-

A man said to me one time that he would be happy, joyous, and successful if God would leave him alone. He really believed that God caused him to suffer. For some reason, he thought that he could run the universe better than the Infinite. He told me, "I hate God for all the failure, trouble, and tragedy that He's brought upon me."

I explained to him that God had nothing to do with his misery and that we experience sickness, suffering, and failure because of our own destructive thinking and misuse of the law of mind. We punish *ourselves* through the natural laws of cause and effect. The punishment ceases when we stop our wrongdoing.

I also pointed out to him it was blasphemy to say that God sends accidents, disease, and pain to us because that's a lie about the Infinite. The truth is that we bring all troubles on ourselves through our own thinking and ignorance of the ways of the Divine Spirit. We shouldn't blame God because *we* make mistakes.

⊶✦⊷

The forces of nature aren't evil; they're neutral. Good and evil are in the way we think and act—not in the things themselves. The wind that blows a ship on the rocks will also bring it to a safe port. However, we do need to learn the laws of navigation. Similarly, electricity itself isn't evil, but we must learn to use it in the right way; otherwise, we may electrocute ourselves and others. Once we understand its principles, we can wire our house and do all manner of wonderful things.

⊶✦⊷

Shakespeare wrote: "There is nothing good or bad, but thinking makes it so." The problem you have at this moment is a wonderful opportunity for you to solve it. There's a wisdom and power within you that will enable you to overcome the difficulty. If you had no challenges in life, you'd never grow. The problem isn't bad and didn't come to plague you; it came to help you release the imprisoned splendor within you. It's a marvelous chance for you to transcend it and prove your capacity because you were born to win. The Infinite is within you and can never fail.

⊶✦⊷

Jerry J., who had severe hearing loss and was going blind, felt bitter and resentful. He asked, "Why did God do this to me?" He felt insecure and inferior. He had great difficulty seeing, and his hearing aid didn't work well and annoyed him. He didn't want his friends to know that he was gradually losing his sight and felt embarrassed when they said to him, "I saw you yesterday at the club, but you never spoke to me." He made excuses, and his resentment and anger about his condition intensified.

I advised Jerry to make a list of all his blessings. He gave thanks for his lovely and faithful wife, his three brilliant daughters, his beautiful home, his marvelous friends, and his kind neighbors. He stopped blaming God and admitted to himself that there were certain people he didn't want to see and certain relatives he didn't want to listen to. He overcame this by blessing and mentally releasing them. His constant prayer was as follows:

> *My vision is spiritual and is a quality of my mind. My eyes are Divine and are always functioning perfectly. My perception of spiritual truth is clear and powerful. The light of understanding dawns in me. I see more and more of God's truth every day. I see better spiritually, mentally, and physically. I see images of truth and beauty everywhere. The Infinite Healing Presence is now—this moment—rebuilding my eyes, which are God's idea. They are perfect Divine instruments that enable me to receive messages from the world within and the world without.*
>
> *The light of God is also revealed in my ears. I hear the truth. I love the truth. I know the truth. My ears are God's perfect idea, functioning perfectly at all times. My ears are the exquisite instruments that reveal God's harmony to me. The love, beauty, and peace of the Infinite flow through my ears. I am in tune with the Divine Presence. I hear the still, small voice of God within me. He quickens my hearing, and my ears are open and free.*

Jerry repeated this affirmation three or four times every morning and night, and gradually these truths sank into his subconscious mind, became active and potent in his life, and released the Healing Presence within him. At the end of a month, his eyesight and hearing had improved remarkably. In fact, he came to see and hear almost normally. His doctors were delighted with his amazing progress. He overcame what he'd heretofore called "evil," and now he's joyous and free.

His story is a reminder that your subconscious takes you literally. When you say, "I hate the sight of someone" or "I don't want to see him or her," your deeper mind takes those statements at face value and proceeds to bring about an occlusion of your vision.

※✝※

It's the will of God that we should all be healthy and happy and lead lives full of marvelous experiences. The Infinite wants us to express more and more wisdom, truth, and beauty. All of us are here to reproduce the qualities, attributes, and potencies of the Healing Presence. Every day of our life, we can advance and move forward in the light. We're here to embody more and more of our Divinity until we become as God intended us: joyous, inspired people who walk the earth with the praise of the Healing Spirit forever on our lips.

※✝※

One reason why many well-meaning people have the strange belief that God's will for them is disaster and unhappiness is that they look upon Him as a hard taskmaster or capricious tyrant living up in the skies, meting out punishment to disobedient children. Of course, that's absurd. God is the Omnipresent Life Principle that wishes you to have greater peace, self-expression, wisdom, prosperity, and love; as well as the capacity to express more light, truth, and beauty. If the will of God for you were sickness, all of the doctors, psychologists, nurses, ministers, priests, and rabbis would be working against God. That's ridiculous!

※✝※

Phineas Parkhurst Quimby, the New Thought pioneer, told a story about a woman who was very ill. Her body was racked with pain, and she said, "It's the will of God that I suffer."

Quimby asked her, "What about your parents? Would they want you to be in agony like this?"

She said, "Oh no! They love me."

Quimby responded, "Why on earth do you attribute greater love to your parents than to the Infinite, which is boundless love, absolute harmony, and perfect peace? All love comes from God, and all the love from parents throughout the world is only a faint echo of His infinite ocean of compassion."

After their conversation, the woman had a great awakening and made a complete recovery.

⊷✞⊶

If you're ill, lonesome, frustrated, bored, or impoverished, you're not expressing the will of the Infinite. But when you unite with God and express His will, you'll experience harmony, vitality, and prosperity. Life's tendency is to express Its own nature, which is love, joy, peace, and beauty. It's the same yesterday, today, and forever. God is absolute harmony and can't wish for sickness or disease. On the contrary, His desire for you transcends your happiest dreams.

⊷✞⊶

It's wrong to say "I'm poor," "I'm sick," "I'm tired," or "I'm broke." When you say these things, you bring these conditions upon yourself by planting negative thoughts in your subconscious that will come forth as experiences and events in your life. Instead, choose Divine guidance, right action, and accomplishment in your life. What's true of the Infinite is true of you, for God dwells within you as the Living Spirit Almighty. God is your life now, and He's always successful, whether making a star, a planet, a tree, or a child. You were born to triumph because the Infinite can't fail.

⌖

You're a choosing, volitional being, not an animal governed by instinct. You have the freedom to love or hate. If you were compelled to love your husband or wife, you'd have no free will. Furthermore, if you were forced to love someone, that wouldn't actually be love.

In order to manifest your choice or desire, you must become enthusiastic about it. Feel the reality of it and pour feeling into it until it becomes embodied in the subconscious mind. In other words, you nourish and exalt your idea and feel the power of the Almighty backing you up. Whatever you give your attention to, your subconscious will magnify and express in your life. *Choose this day whom you will serve.*

When you learn to choose wisely, you'll choose happiness, peace, security, joy, health, abundance, and all the blessings of life instead of sickness, lack, or limitation. You'll begin to know the great truths and find the kingdom of God within yourself. You'll enthrone the Divine values in your mind until they become a part of your consciousness.

⌖

You'll see a world that is governed by appearances and conditions until you awaken to the fact that you can control and direct your life by using your own thoughts and feelings. Gradually you'll understand the truth that circumstances and events are effects—not causes—and are subject to change. As you change your mind, you'll transform your body, environment, and life.

⌖

There are some people who are victims of the mass mind and unconsciously choose disease, misfortune, and scarcity. They say,

"I've been jinxed," "Everything is against me," "I'm going to fail," "I'm getting the flu," and this sort of thing. They fail to realize that thoughts are things and that what they imagine, they become; and what they feel, they attract.

If you don't do your own thinking, the media, the neighbors, and the mass mind (six billion people) will do your thinking for you. And your life will be a mess. What did you focus on this morning or this afternoon? What kind of thoughts did you choose? Make sure that you don't adopt the thinking of the many people who believe that the will of the Infinite is something unpleasant or bad. Say this prayer several times each day:

> *God is boundless love, absolute bliss, indescribable beauty, and supreme peace. There are no divisions in the Infinite, which is perfect. God's eyes are too pure to behold inequity. God's will is being made manifest in my life as Divine harmony, health, happiness, abundance, and love.*

If you meditate on these words regularly, your present circumstances will "magically" be transformed into the likeness of what you're contemplating. Now when you say, "God's will is operating in my life," it has a magnificent and beautiful meaning. All of the good things in life are intended for you, but you must open your mind to receive them. Accept the gift that has been proffered since the foundation of time.

☙✙❧

"God's will be done" is a magnificent prayer, particularly when you understand the spiritual significance of these words. If you enthrone in your mind the definite idea that God's will is operating in all your affairs, this constructive belief will govern your life. When you know that the light of God is guiding you in all your ways, you're automatically protected from making errors and unwise decisions and wasting your time and effort on useless endeavors.

※✝※

I've frequently heard the expression "I want it if God wants me to have it." That's superstition! What is it that God *doesn't* want you to have? God is the Giver and the Gift. God gave you Himself. The Divine Presence is in your own subjective depths, and the whole world is yours. If you really believe that God is the Life within you and that Infinite Intelligence is boundless love, why should you think that God doesn't want you to have something? It's already been given to you, and you must accept it. The gift of God is health, peace, joy, abundance, a new home, and anything else that is good. All of this is for you.

You're here to reproduce all the qualities, potencies, and aspects of the One Who Forever Is and to move from glory to glory. If you have a desire for healing, true expression, greater wisdom, spiritual understanding, or abundant wealth, surely there isn't a doubt in your mind that the Infinite Presence and Power wants you to have all these things, too. What kind of a God wouldn't want you to free, joyous, and illumined? If you think that God wants you to be sick or is testing you in some strange way, such a god isn't worthy of your consideration and attention. That kind of belief is only a superstitious concept in your mind.

※✝※

Many people, because of false theological beliefs that were implanted in their subconscious mind when they were young and impressionable, believe that it's virtuous to suffer from lack and limitation. This is completely wrong. Poverty is a curse and a disease of the mind. It has a bad odor. You must eradicate that false belief from your subconscious and realize that the infinite riches of God are all around you. God gave you everything to enjoy.

Everywhere you look you see a profusion of God's abundance. You can't count the grains of sand on the seashore or the stars in the heavens above. Have you ever tried to count the flowers as you drove along the road? His ideas are infinite, and you could have one now that could make you rich and put a million people to work. Ideas are wealth. So is a book, a new business venture, or a real-estate project.

Nature is lavish, extravagant, and bountiful. Because of greed, we create artificial shortages, but there are no limits to God's wisdom and creative ideas. There's no lack of energy, for energy is Spirit, which is inexhaustible and eternal. It was never born and will never die. You need to open your mind and be receptive to the Divine influx that's always ready and available.

Believe that your supply is from God, the Living Spirit within you. This God Presence meets all of your needs at every moment. The external world, economic conditions, stock-market fluctuations, inflation, and the opinions of others can't touch you when you're lifted up in consciousness. Be completely free in your economic thinking and you'll prosper in all your ways.

⌘

You're not glorifying the Infinite when you're sick, frustrated, neurotic, unhappy, or poor. You must demonstrate your faith in God and His riches. It must manifest in your home, body, art, science, business, and all aspects of your life. You're here to express in the Infinite in your life, for faith without works is dead.

To believe in a God of love is to express love, and to believe in a God of abundance is to create an abundant life. If you have a desire to write a play, start a business, or build a new house, wouldn't it be extremely foolish for you to think that God didn't will these things? God is within you, and your desire to create comes from God, Who speaks to you through desire. If you're sick, you have a desire for health, which is the Healing Presence's wish.

God gave you your mind, the urge to achieve, and the intelligence to do all these things. If God gave you a voice, you don't ask, "Is it God's will that I sing?" Good heavens—go forth and sing!

Imagine saying, "If God wants me to write a play, he'll let me know." Nothing could be more absurd. Your idea or desire must be planted in your mind and felt as true. Then the subconscious will bring it to pass. That's the law of mind. Your conscious desire has now passed from mere wishful thinking to become a subconscious conviction. In other words, if you want something—health, a contract, a home, or whatever it might be—Infinite Spirit will open up the way for the perfect development of that idea. Like a seed, It attracts everything necessary for its fruition. Your ideas come to you from God, Who clears a path for you. Then you see the finished product and can hear your spouse or friends congratulating you on the marvelous success of your invention. How wonderful it is!

⌖

John P. came to see me some years ago. He was an alcoholic and said that if he had one drink, he'd be compelled to keep on drinking until he fell unconscious on the floor. In other words, he'd lost control and was compelled by the law of his subconscious mind to overindulge.

His story was a familiar one. His wife had divorced him because of his infidelity, and he'd gotten angry and hated her because she refused to take him back. He then turned to alcohol to relieve the pain. Each time he took a drink to bolster his spirits, he was rejecting the power of the Infinite within him. Instead, he was planting ideas of weakness and inferiority in his subconscious. He began to increase the amount he drank. In the beginning he had a choice. He could choose to have two, three, or four drinks, and that was it. But he lost control and now when he had one drink, he was off to the races.

He'd established the idea in his mind that he needed to drink to excess. The nature of the subconscious is compulsion. Whatever is impressed upon it is brought forth as form, experience, and event. It's very simple.

Fortunately, John reversed the pattern and freed himself by the use of the same law that made him a compulsive drinker. Regularly and systematically, he contemplated freedom and peace of mind, claiming that his food and drink were God's ideas that brought him harmony, health, and joy. He ran a movie in his mind several times daily, imagining himself as free and happy. He pictured himself doing what he longed to do and hearing a friend congratulate him on his sobriety and peace of mind. Whenever he was tempted to drink, he flashed this movie in his mind, knowing that the power of the Almighty was flowing through him and that the mental image of health was sinking down into his subconscious, where it was developed in the darkroom of his mind.

Impressions are made on the subconscious by repetition, faith, and expectancy. As John continued faithfully imagining his freedom and peace of mind, the dawn came and all the shadows flew away. His conscious will—desire for freedom from a destructive habit—became his subconscious will, meaning a deep, abiding conviction lodged in his deeper mind. He was compelled to express freedom, for the law of the subconscious is compulsion.

⊨✢⊨

When you were young, you were probably given taboos, restrictions, and a series of "don'ts." When you were sick, maybe you were told that it was God's will or that He was punishing you for behaving badly. These are things that parents still teach their children today. When I was little, I was told that if I didn't go to church or say my prayers, something bad would happen to me. These are frightful beliefs. Awful! They contaminate and pollute the soul. They're based on gross ignorance and superstition.

Perhaps you were told that a lake of fire was waiting for you. Imagine someone saying to you that if you don't believe in a particular creed, you'll burn for all eternity. What kind of love is that? Would you want anyone to suffer forever? If you do, there's no love in your life.

God is pure compassion, and a lake of fire has never existed. There are only fires of vengeance, hate, and hostility operating in the human mind, destroying our peace and health. We have lost our reason and are punishing ourselves. These are the gangsters that bedevil our minds, but love will cast them out. Realize that God wouldn't do anything unloving because He's absolute compassion, harmony, and bliss, the only Presence and Power.

‑⊶⊹⊷‑

"Thy will be done on Earth as it is in heaven" is a wonderful prayer when you understand its meaning. *Heaven* means your own mind, or mental and spiritual awareness. It signifies the Infinite Intelligence within your being. You'll experience on Earth what you feel is true in the heaven of your own mind. *Earth,* the objective plane, is your body, world, environment, wallet, circumstances, profession, and all aspects of your life. *Will* is your capacity to define your objectives or choose your goals.

Give your desires your attention and devotion, and finally they'll gel within you. Your desert blooms as a paradise, and your will becomes God's will or the joy of an answered prayer. God didn't give you a spirit of fear, but the power of love and a sound mind. Each day is a time of renewal, resurgence, and rebirth. All nature proclaims the glory of a new day.

You must awaken the God Presence within, arise from your long sleep of limitation, and walk in the morning of a new day and a new life. Fear, ignorance and superstition will die as you resurrect faith, confidence, love, and goodwill.

Begin now to take the following transfusion of God's grace and love. Say to yourself with feeling:

I am filled with the cleansing, harmonizing, vitalizing life of the Holy Spirit. My body is a temple of the Living God. It is pure, whole, and perfect. Every function of my mind and body is governed by Divine wisdom and order. God in the midst of me is mighty to heal. God's peace fills my soul, and God's love saturates my entire being. The Healing Presence in me is guiding me now.

In a Nutshell

God is Life with no beginning or end. It always seeks to express Itself through us as beauty, joy, harmony, love, wisdom, and order.

It's God's will that we should all be healthy and joyous; lead lives full of marvelous experiences; and express more and more wisdom, truth, and beauty. We're here to express more of our Divinity every day until we become the inspired, happy people that God intended us to be, walking the Earth with the praise of the Healing Presence forever on our lips.

The forces of nature aren't evil; they're neutral. Good and evil are in the way we think and act and the attitude we take toward things—not in the things themselves.

Remember that you're a volitional being, not an animal governed by instinct. You have choice and the freedom to love. *Choose this day whom you will serve.*

You're not glorifying the Infinite when you're sick, frustrated, neurotic, unhappy, or poor. You must demonstrate your faith in God and His riches. You're here to create what you really believe in and express in your life what is true of the Infinite.

It's a magnificent prayer to say, "God's will be done," particularly when you understand the spiritual significance of these words. If you enthrone in your mind the definite idea that God's will is operating in all of your affairs, this constructive belief will govern your life.

Your dominant conviction dictates your entire life. When you know that the light and love of God is guiding you in all your ways, you're automatically protected from making errors in judgment and wasting your time and effort on useless endeavors.

When you focus on your desire and rejoice in it, realizing that the Almighty Power is backing you up, it will gradually gel in your subconscious mind. Like a seed, it will blossom as the joy of an answered prayer.

Chapter Four

The Fourth Way to Pray

The book of Daniel tells the story of how King Nebuchadnezzar condemned the Jewish men Shadrach, Meshach, and Abed-Nego to burn in a fiery furnace for refusing to worship the gold image he'd erected in Babylon. However, although the men were bound and put in the fire, not a hair on their heads was singed.

The Bible says: "Then King Nebuchadnezzar was astonished; and he rose in haste and spoke, saying to his counselors, 'Did we not cast three men bound into the midst of the fire?' They answered and said to the king, 'True, O king.' 'Look!' he answered, 'I see four men loose, walking in the midst of the fire; and they are not hurt, and the form of the fourth is like the Son of God.'"

The fourth man in the furnace is the consciousness of God, your awareness of the Living Spirit Almighty within you. When you're in tune with the Infinite—in a higher spiritual dimension—fire can't burn you and poison can't kill you.

Shadrach, Meshach, and Abed-Nego represent faith, love, and understanding. *Faith*, of course, means your definite belief that the Infinite Intelligence responds when you call upon It. *Love* in the Bible means loyalty and devotion to the One Power, for there's no other. You need to put the Creator first in your life. *Understanding* means your insight into the workings of the law of mind and your trust that whatever you believe in your heart will come to pass.

The "Fourth Way" to pray is to contemplate the Presence of God or the Infinite within you that can't be divided or multiplied. The Fourth Way encompasses all the knowledge of science, philosophy, and religion—plus an awareness and exalted recognition of the Presence of God in humankind.

※✝※

I read a scientific paper about the experience of a clairvoyant woman who had a vision of an airplane coming out of the clouds in flames. It burned out about 100 feet from the ground, then cracked and fell. She knew that this disaster was going to take place as well as the location and the time it would happen. However, she couldn't see the faces of the two men in the plane, which were charred beyond recognition.

This woman went to a friend's house overlooking the field where the plane was to come down. At half past two, she asked her friend to go outside and help her. The two stood there praying. Suddenly the airplane that she'd seen in her vision appeared in flames. It cracked and plummeted to the ground, just as she'd foreseen. But the two men in the plane were absolutely unharmed. It was like the case of Shadrach, Meshach, and Abed-Nego—they weren't even singed.

One of the men said, "I was about to throw myself out of the plane when suddenly a sense of absolute peace and safety came over and I sat back down." That man turned out to be the son of the clairvoyant's friend.

The two women prayed by practicing the Presence of God where the plane was. In other words, they contemplated love, peace, harmony, beauty, and Divine right action. In their minds and hearts, they immersed the two men in the Holy Omnipresence. They saw them bathed in the light of God and succeeded in saving their lives. Had the women had a 100 percent realization of the Infinite, they could have saved the plane, too.

※✝※

In 1935 and 1936, the English Society for Psychical Research ran a series of tests on two Indian fakirs in Surrey, England. Physicians, chemists, physicists, and psychologists from Oxford and Cambridge evaluated the study. The Indians walked on fire under controlled conditions, observed by the skeptical and probing eyes of science. The surface temperatures were between 4,500 and 5,000 degrees Celsius, and the interior temperature of the fire was approximately 14,000 degrees. They repeated the experiment under a variety of conditions over a period of several weeks. There was no trickery or hallucination involved.

A high point was reached when one of the fakirs noticed that a professor of psychology was intrigued and dumbfounded. Sensing his longing, the Indian man told the professor that he, too, could walk the fire if he so desired—by holding his hand. The professor was seized with faith that he could. He shed his shoes and hand in hand, they walked the fire ecstatic and unharmed.

Faith is an attitude of mind. It's belief in the One Creative Power that responds to you when you call upon It. Everyone knows that fire burns, but when you tune in to the Infinite and reach a high state of consciousness, you become immune.

※✝※

Not many people know that Virginia Graham's success in her famous TV show *Girl Talk* happened after she beat terminal cancer and made medical history. Her doctor explained the miracle. He said that Virginia purified her bloodstream with her thoughts. She prayed consistently and knew that she would be healed and live. "I have a surviving point of view," she stated.

This love of life communicates itself and is probably one of the reasons for her wonderful TV career. Although she was given a terminal diagnosis, she decided to believe something different and established a new construct in her mind. An altered state of consciousness brought about the healing. She lived for another 40 years, dying in 1998 at the age of 86.

You may have a solid knowledge of science and philosophy and be devoutly religious, but this kind of understanding fails time and again to help men and women solve their problems. What you need to do is turn to the Supreme Intelligence within—as Virginia did—and let that Presence and Power coordinate all your activities and direct your life along a glorious path.

⊯✝⊭

When Charles Lindbergh made the first solo nonstop flight across the Atlantic Ocean, he was a pioneer. He didn't have a co-pilot, radio, or parachute; and he was guided only by a compass. During the flight, he experienced the functioning of the Higher Power within him, which controlled his mind and body and directed the flight and prodded him to activity when necessary. When his conscious, reasoning mind was suspended in sleep, he became aware of transparent forms riding with him. He felt that he was guided by benevolent Beings who were very friendly and gave him valuable information on navigation—reassuring and comforting him all the way. His subconscious mind took over while he was sound asleep.

Lindbergh couldn't focus his attention on his route through-out the flight, yet when he awakened, he sighted Ireland, and was only a few miles off his course when he had a fourth-dimensional experience that saved his life. That's the Fourth Way to pray.

Learn as much about science and other matters as you can and find a religion you believe in, but when you meet with some great difficulty and find that all you know can't solve it, turn to the Divine Presence within, knowing in your heart that It is all-wise, omnipotent, and supreme. It knows only the answer, and before you call, It responds to you.

⛊

When World War I fighter pilot Eddie Rickenbacker was adrift on a raft in the ocean, he called on the Universal Presence and Power. Then a gull flew down to provide food for him, and rain fell to quench his thirst. He was protected and rescued in Divine order. His knowledge of science and religion didn't save him, but he called on the Healing Presence in his time of trouble, and It answered him.

⛊

Some theologians talk *about* God instead of teaching men and women to experience God in their own hearts. These religious thinkers and leaders are usually good, kind people and follow all the rules and regulations of their churches. They believe in a personal savior and so on. However, they often suffer miserably. The truth is that you're your own savior and answer your own prayers. Whatever you impress on your subconscious is expressed as form, function, experience, and event. If you don't know that, you're living in the Dark Ages. The law of mind is: "As a man thinketh in his heart [or subconscious], so is he."

⛊

Dogmatism means to assert something without evidence—to claim something that every scientist knows is false, such as "the world was created in six days" or "Adam and Eve were the first parents." Those stories are just parables. Adam and Eve represent your conscious and subconscious mind, respectively. The harmonious interaction of your subconscious and conscious mind brings forth health, happiness, peace, abundance, and security.

⛊

We've had horrific wars down through the ages and will continue to experience them until we awaken to the Presence and Power of God within us and realize that the six billion people in this world are simply extensions of ourselves, for there's only One Mind. Then we we'll know that whatever we wish for or think, we're creating in our own minds, bodies, pocketbooks and circumstances. When we understand this simple truth, we'll pour forth our benediction on all humankind. We won't want to deceive, rob, or cheat anyone. There will be no avarice in our hearts because we'll know that whatever we can claim and feel to be true, Infinite Spirit manifests.

⊶✚⊷

What you really believe in your heart is what you experience. If you believe in failure, even if you work very hard, you won't succeed. You might be kind to the poor, visit sick people in the hospital, and tithe, but it's what you believe in your heart that manifests—not what you give theoretical assent to. It's your emotional espousals that express themselves. For example, a person may go to church every day and receive sacraments, but if he expects setbacks or fears the flu or failure, he'll experience all these things. The law of the Lord is perfect, and you can't think negatively and get good results.

⊶✚⊷

Many people may score 100 percent in their philosophical examination and can quote Plato, Aristotle, and Emerson; yet their lives are chaotic. You see, they haven't assimilated or incorporated these philosophical ideas into their subconscious mind. Head knowledge isn't *heart* knowledge. If you truly digest the ideas of Emerson, you'll be walking in the light and you'll experience the moment that lasts forever.

᪣✛᪣

A doctor who served in Vietnam told me that during an emergency, he'd had to parachute out of his plane and found himself wounded and alone in the jungle. He began to pray: "I know God or Spirit is within me. It's all-wise and is leading me to safety now." He said that he knew that Infinite Intelligence would respond.

A few minutes later, his brother appeared to him and said, "I will order the medics to come for you. They'll be here in half an hour." And within 30 minutes, the medics did arrive on the scene and rescued him.

He asked the doctors, "How did you know I was here?" They explained that an officer had appeared and given them the precise directions to find him. Their description of the officer exactly fit his brother—who'd been killed in action the year before. This is the Fourth Way. The answer comes in ways you can't conceive of.

᪣✛᪣

According to the Bible, when Daniel was in the lions' den, he turned his back on the beasts and turned toward the Light within. The lions were then powerless to hurt him. The story of Daniel is about all people everywhere, including you. The lions represent the seemingly insurmountable problems in life. When faced with a threatening situation, Daniel turned his back on the lions and looked for an escape through the Power of the Almighty within him.

When many people have a challenge, they look at it, argue about it, talk about it, and magnify it—and then it engulfs them. Don't do that. Turn away from your difficulty like Daniel did. Concentrate on receiving a solution through the Power of the Almighty. Focus your attention on that, and claim and feel the reality of your desire. As you continue to do so, God will respond and move on your behalf.

⊣⊹⊢

I remember a soldier telling me that during a battle, bullets were flying all around him, coming from every direction. He said, "The only thing I could remember was a prayer I learned at my mother's knee. He said he didn't even know the meaning of this prayer but could recall a few verses: "The Lord is my shepherd, I shall not want. He maketh me to lie down in green pastures. He restoreth my soul."

He remembered these few words and in his desperation, he turned to the One Power. All of a sudden, lightning flashed in the sky, followed by an immense storm with rain coming down in torrents. The bullets ceased, and he found his way to safety. This was the response of Infinite Intelligence.

⊣⊹⊢

Your desire for freedom from your problem is a seed that you deposit in your subconscious mind, confident that it shall blossom to its full potential. Don't worry or be anxious about *how* the answer comes, as the ways of your subconscious are beyond finding out. Your consciousness, or awareness, is the only Presence and Power . . . the Eternal Cause of all creation.

Create a new mental attitude, and a new Earth will appear. Know that God is always there in times of trouble and remember these words from Psalm 91: "He who dwells in the shelter of the Most High will rest in the shadow of the Almighty. I will say of the Lord, 'He is my refuge and my fortress, my God, in whom I trust.' . . . He will cover you with his feathers, and under his wings you will find refuge; his faithfulness will be your shield and rampart. . . . I will be with him in trouble, I will deliver him and honor him."

In a Nutshell

The Fourth Way to pray is to contemplate the Presence of God, or the Infinite within you, which can't be divided or multiplied.

When you meet with some great problem and find that all you know can't solve it, turn to the Divine Presence within, knowing in your heart that It is all-wise, omnipotent, and supreme. It knows only the answer, and before you call on It, the solution is provided. It is the Absolute Intelligence.

The Fourth Way encompasses all the knowledge of science, philosophy, and religion—plus an awareness and exalted recognition of the Presence of God in humankind.

Whatever we wish or think about another, we create in our own minds, bodies, wallets, and circumstances. When we awaken to this simple truth, we'll pour forth our benediction on all humankind. We won't want to deceive, rob, or cheat anyone. There will be no avarice in our hearts because we'll realize that whatever we can claim and feel to be true, Spirit will give to us.

What you really believe in your heart is what you experience. If you believe in failure, even if you work very hard, you won't succeed. You might be kind to the poor, visit hospitals, tithe, and do many charitable things, but it's what you believe in your heart that manifests—not what you give theoretical assent to. It's not your nominal belief but your conviction in your heart that matters.

When many people have a problem, they argue about it, talk about it, and magnify it—and then it engulfs them. Instead, remove your attention from your troubles. Concentrate on receiving a solution through the Power of the Almighty. As you do so, God will respond.

⛪ ⛪

Chapter Five

Science and Religion

Some years ago, Dr. Charles Littlefield, a distinguished scientist, tried to create life. He succeeded in showing that organic life-forms can spontaneously emerge from chemicals, but he realized that nobody can create life, which already exists. Life is God and has no beginning or end. It was never born and will never die.

Dr. Littlefield also uncovered the truth of the biblical statement: "As a man thinketh in his heart [subconscious mind], so is he." While researching in his lab, he discovered that his focused thought took form. One day when he was working with a saline solution under a microscope, he concentrated his attention on a frail, elderly lady in the room. He stood gazing intently at her for some time. When he turned back to look at the saline solution, he was surprised to find an image of a miniature form of this woman in his microscope. Day after day, he concentrated on certain mental pictures, and he was amazed to see his mental imagery take form in the shapes developed by the crystals in the saline solution.

Littlefield's discovery provides further evidence that we become what we think about all day long. After all, our thoughts are the tools that shape our destiny. They can even be photographed. They have form and structure in our brains; and they're gradually being condensed into cells, blood, and tissue as well as manifesting as experiences, events, and conditions.

⊶✝⊷

I read an article in which someone asked Einstein what matter is. He replied that it's "energy reduced to the point of visibility." *Energy* is a term used by scientists for Spirit, which of course is God. As it was said in the Upanishad ten thousand years ago: "Matter is the lowest degree of Spirit, and Spirit is the highest degree of matter." Today a revolution is taking place in the fields of chemistry and physics. We now know that everything is energy, vibrations, and frequencies. Scientists are proving that we're living in a dynamic, evolving universe. Everything is alive, and energy and mass are one.

⊶✝⊷

Some scientists in the 19th century were under the impression that all of the great discoveries in physics had already been made. They said that all that was left to do was to make more exact quantitative measurements. However, we can't measure love with a ruler or weigh it on a scale. How could we quantify peace, beauty, wisdom, or inspiration? We can't do so because we're dealing with the intangible and the invisible.

When you lift a chair, it's the Unseen Power acting—not your arms. You also can't see the Power that propels your fingers to write. Surely you don't think that they move themselves! It's the Creative Spirit within that propels all the actions of your body; and your thoughts, emotions, and imagery direct this Spirit.

⊶✝⊷

People who take the Bible literally believe that God created the world in six days and rested on the seventh. This is only a parable, however. Geologists, paleontologists, archaeologists, anthropologists, physicists, astronomers, and other scientists realize that the cosmos took millions of years to assume the form it now has. This evolution took place in Divine order according to an archetypal design of Infinite Intelligence, which is the only Creative Power.

Unless we understand the symbolic essence of scripture, we actually have no Bible at all. For example, the story of creation in Genesis can be seen as representing the prayer process: *Six days* refers to the length of time it takes to impregnate the subconscious with a wish or idea. However, we shouldn't take this literally—it might take us a minute, an hour, or several weeks. As soon as we succeed in planting the seeds of our desire, we can have a day of rest because we're no longer seeking what we already have. This is the Sabbath, the seventh day on which we know that our prayer has been answered. It has nothing to do with the days of the week.

⊶✦⊷

Judge Troward, who lived in India for many years, was a great student of all the religions of the world and was a marvelous, intuitive individual. He wrote many textbooks on the power of the mind. In 1900, he described the evolution of the Earth:

> The physical history of our planet shows us first an incandescent nebula dispersed over vast infinitudes of space. Later this condensed into a central sum surrounded by a family of glowing planets hardly yet consolidated from the plastic primordial matter. Then succeed untold millennia of slow geological formations. And Earth peopled by the lowest forms of life, whether vegetable or animal, from which crude beginnings a majestic, unceasing, unhurried forward movement brings things stage by stage to the conditions in which we know them now.

A great number of modern scientists today agree with what Troward wrote more than 100 years ago. Indeed, he had an intuitive understanding of the truths of the Bible.

※✛※

Sir James Jeans, an English physicist and astronomer who was knighted for his work, said that after 40 years of research he was convinced that the whole universe is simply a thought in the mind of an Infinite Being. Indeed, thousands of years ago in the Upanishad, it was written that God thinks, causing worlds to appear. We're living in an ever-changing, evolving universe of dancing forces; and the entire world is a mental phenomenon.

※✛※

In medical circles, it's customary to discard the textbooks of yesterday's pathologies and nostrums. Likewise, we must throw out old superstitions and false beliefs about an avenging God, hell, the devil, and evil forces—the language and verbiage of times past. We need to understand that the belief in eternal damnation was created by our ancestors out of their ignorance and lack of understanding.

Let go of these antiquated ideas and become an open-minded seeker of truth. When you say that God is punishing you or that He'll judge you on the "last day," you must ask yourself: *Where did such an idea come from? Who said it? Why was it said? What's the origin of it? Is there any sense or meaning in it? Is it contrary to the laws of life and the way of the Spirit? Is it illogical, unreasonable, and unscientific? Have I been brainwashed since my youth? Am I a victim of ignorance, superstition, and fear?*

In fact, there's only One Presence, which is light and awareness. According to modern science, everything is light and vibration—even your body is made up of waves of light.

※✛※

In ancient times, prehistoric people realized that they were subject to forces over which they had no control. The sun gave scorched the Earth, fire burned them, and water flooded their land and drowned the cattle. They conceived of external gods who could reward or punish them, and they divided the deities into two categories: beneficent and malignant powers. Based on this crude reasoning, they set about making offerings and sacrifices to the gods to try to prevent disasters and protect themselves. Thus, love and fear gave rise to the earliest religions.

Of course, we know today that there's only One Power. When we use It constructively, harmoniously, and peacefully, we call It *God, health,* and *happiness.* When we use It ignorantly or maliciously, we call It the *devil, misery, misfortune,* and so on.

᪥᪥᪥

Just as chemistry, physics, and astronomy are sciences, there's also a "Divine science." It's a practical teaching that you can use to get results. The law of mind is: If you think positively, good follows; and if you think negatively, you'll reap unpleasant results.

Your deep-seated beliefs govern you. Whatever idea or thought is dominant in your subconscious mind takes control of your thoughts, actions, and reactions. If you believe that you're jinxed or doomed, you can't succeed. You can work 18 hours a day, but you'll still fail because negativity is the focus of your mind. In the same way, if you believe that the weather gives you a cold, you've installed a false belief that governs your reality. On the other hand, you can enthrone in your mind ideas of harmony, health, peace, and joy and create a very happy existence. What's the preeminent idea in *your* mind? *According to your belief is it done unto you.*

᪥᪥᪥

Great scientists realize that there's an Infinite Spirit that governs everything. All of these distinguished thinkers—many of whom are Nobel Prize winners—are mystics who intuitively perceive the great truths of God. As Arthur Thompson, one of the world's notable scientists, said: "There can be nothing in this world that can exist apart from God, and no Power that is not ultimately His." The center of religion, he said, is a belief in a reality beyond the everyday world.

⌗✛⌗

Albert Cliff, a distinguished Canadian chemist, wrote:

> The whole world has become increasingly food conscious, with our leading magazines and journals publishing many articles on nutrition by specialists, most of them advising us to eat the food we ought to eat instead of the food we like to eat. The word "vitamins" is flung at us from every conceivable angle with warnings of the dreadful things that will happen to us should we not heed their importance.
>
> As a food chemist, I know that the foods I eat each day are converted to the various parts of my body. In other words, my physical well-being depends for its development upon my daily intake. However, several years ago, it was found that in spite of having a so-called perfect diet, many people suffered from diseases which, according to the principles of nutrition, should never have occurred. It was then that I came into the study of the mind, which has taught me that the food I give to my mind each hour and each day is of far greater importance than the foods I give to my stomach. The words of the Bible are applicable: "Be not, therefore, anxious what ye shall eat or what ye shall drink." By an application of these words, I discovered that I alone was the cause of my intense suffering from stomach ulcers for 27 years.

Once I proved that my mental vitamins were the real source of my sickness or health, I became as I wished to be—healthy, happy and successful.

Cliff is saying that although eating healthfully is important, the most important food is what you're feeding your *mind*. If you're angry, resentful, or hateful, you can eat the choicest food and the best vitamins and minerals and they'll still turn into cancer, arthritis, lumbago, and every disease under the sun. You are what you eat mentally and spiritually.

⊯✝⊱

Einstein once said, "The most beautiful and most profound emotion you can experience is the sensation of the mystical. It is the power of all true science. One to whom this emotion is a stranger, who can no longer wonder and stand wrapped in awe, is as good as dead. What is impenetrable to us really exists, manifesting itself as the highest wisdom and the most radiant beauty, which our dull faculties can comprehend only in their most primitive form. This knowledge, this feeling, is the center of true religion."

When most scientists refer to the *mysteries of the universe,* they avoid using the word *God.* Yet Einstein had no such inhibitions. He said, "My religion consists of a humble admiration of the unlimited Spirit, which reveals itself in the slight details we are able to perceive with our frail and feeble minds."

⊯✝⊱

Dr. Donald Andrews, who served as a professor of chemistry at Johns Hopkins University, wrote:

> During the last 25 years, studies with a spectroscope, and particularly with a diffraction apparatus, have given us startling answers to the question: "Who am I?" As

we look and listen [at an enlargement of an atom of calcium], we see, first of all, ripples and waves moving around the electrons like the ripples and waves in a pond when a storm passes through it. [Using sophisticated audio devices] we hear a humming like a hive of bees. We become aware of overwhelming music all around us. Although hitherto we have been completely unaware of the waves of sound, we realize that we are listening to a vast symphony. The range of tone extends many octaves beyond anything we have ever heard in a concert hall. We detect chords that are sometimes familiar, yet part of a vaster pattern that goes beyond any music ever dreamed of in a human brain. As this music surges around us, we come to realize that it is here in these patterns of harmony, melody, and counterpoint that we have the true reality, the essence of what it is that creates what we see, what we feel, and what we are. Thus, through the magic eyes and ears of science, we behold the vision of this previously unseen and unheard realm. We are tuned to the music of the spheres.

Of course, Dr. Andrews is proving what the ancient mystics said: "God sings a song, and that song is humankind." The universe itself is one song, and every single thing you see is the thought of God made manifest. Your body is simply waves of Divine light.

Dr. Andrews notes, "If we can keep throughout our lives a vivid sense of the reality of the Spirit and the vision of the Invisible Kingdom within us, then we can go forward confidently into this new atomic age on the road to a high destiny. And when humankind finally establishes peace and goodwill on Earth, we will understand at last the deepest meaning of the biblical words: 'You shall know the truth, and the truth shall set you free.'"

⇥✝⇤

The principle of your subconscious is impersonal; therefore, you can have what you impress in your deeper mind—whether it's good or bad. That's the law of mind. It's the nature of an apple seed to become an apple tree, and it's inevitable that the seeds you plant in your subconscious will manifest in every area of your life. Whatever you really believe comes into your experience. What kind of crop are *you* sowing?

⊶✢⊷

What you receive depends on the size of the container you use. For example, you can go to the ocean to gather water in a thimble or in a bathtub—the ocean doesn't care. There's always the same amount of water in the world. In your life, your mind and heart are the container. Open them wide to receive all the blessings of life that are already waiting for you. The cattle on a thousand hills, all the apples on the trees, and every other single thing in the universe are here waiting for you to receive them.

Consider whether you're a good receiver. Many people aren't. You can only take what you really believe you can have and nothing more. You'll automatically attract according to the conviction of your mind. This is referred to as the *law of mental equivalents*. For instance, some people may regard a million-dollar income as normal. To others, the amount is inconceivable and they can't even imagine it. Still other individuals receive tens of millions of dollars every year. What you receive depends completely on your mental attitude. Your subconscious mind responds according to the level of your expectancy or belief. Furthermore, you can't escape your own thoughts and imagery because you become what you think about all day long.

⊶✢⊷

You can wish for many things, such as a first-class trip around the world. However, the desire alone won't make it happen. You may want to climb to a mountaintop but say, "It's too high. I have sore feet and am too old now." Well, with that attitude, of course you'll never get there. But constructive thinkers look at the same mountain and say, "I'm going toward my vision." Naturally, these people succeed. They may get blisters but they reach their goal.

You see, "wishers" aren't achievers. Your wish must become a *conviction*. For example, a movie director spent a few nights meditating on a certain story idea, thinking about it from all angles. He considered the setting, the characters, and the tone. On the third night, the impulse came to him to write. The idea took over, and he wrote a play that he sold for $50,000.

Where was the wealth? In his mind. The subconscious gave him everything. It brought forth the plot, the characters, and everything else. That's the way all great inventions and writing comes about—from the depths and conviction of the deeper mind.

⋇

Raise your sights and strike out for the good life. You can stay in the valley or climb the mountain. The Spirit is supreme and It is within you. It is the Eternal Source of all things. Divorce your thinking from the mass mind by asking yourself, "What are the six billion people in the world thinking?" Many are full of hate, resentment, and hostility and are contemplating murder. Surely, there's *some* good, you say. Yes, millions of people are thinking constructively and harmoniously, but they're in the minority. The mass mind believes in tragedy, accidents, misfortunes, disease, and all sorts of negative things.

If you don't do your own thinking, then the world mind will do it for you. If you have any fear, worry, or self-condemnation, it's the mass mind thinking in you, kicking you around like a football. Do you own your own mind? Or are your in-laws or the media manipulating you? You're only truly thinking when you think from the standpoint of universal principles and eternal verities, contemplating the truths of God from the highest standpoint. Then you're a spiritual innovator because you're not entertaining the same old thoughts that your grandfather or some theologian had.

⊞✠⊞

Spirit is perfect, and It flows through everything. Look at a leaf on a tree; it's precisely shaped. So are the blades of grass, the birds, and the fish in the sea. They function perfectly. Electrons and protons are also exquisite. They join together and separate according to Divine law.

Why not begin to focus on the Infinite Spirit within you instead of thinking about all the imperfections in the world? If you're dwelling on the shortcomings of other people, you're creating lack in your own mind, body, and pocketbook. If you're jealous of someone, you're demeaning and impoverishing yourself. You're putting the other person on a pedestal and saying, "You have the power to disturb me. You can have all the good things in life, but I can't." You're then denying your own Divinity and affirming lack and limitation. You're poisoning your own food and then eating it. That's why jealousy is called the "green-eyed monster."

⊞✠⊞

If you take a teaspoon of ink and put it into five gallons of distilled water, it will color all the liquid to some degree. In the same way, you infuse everything with your beliefs and opinions. If you're fearful or hateful, then every person and thing that comes into your experience is tinted by that attitude of mind. If you have an inferiority complex, you project your self-criticism onto members of your family. You don't like what you see, but it's actually within *you.*

As the ancients said, we don't see the world as it is, but as *we* are. We see everything through the prism of our conditioning, early training, theological concepts, and beliefs. For example, two women look at a drunkard in the gutter. One sees the Presence of God and says, "God's love fills his mind and heart; God's peace floods his mind." The other woman comments, "They should use him in scientific experimentation instead of guinea pigs or mice." Now, the two women see the same man, but each looks through the lens of her own mentality.

Similarly, a husband and wife can have different reactions to Niagara Falls. She says, "You know, I could never come back here because I just don't like it," He looks at the thundering water and exclaims, "It's marvelous, inspiring, and beautiful! I'm coming back every year." The wife's mental reaction is distaste, while the husband's is pleasure.

※✦※

One young woman told me that her boss was sadistic and seemed to delight in irritating people. She said that she hated him so much that she couldn't even stand the way he smoked his pipe. It's easy to see how this happened. She identified with her supervisor's negative aspects until his voice, his clothes, and everything about him—including his pipe—were colored by her reaction.

When I pointed out that she had no responsibility for his actions, but only for her own, she began to see the light. I explained that it isn't what happens to us but our thought or reaction to it that's important. I told her that since feelings follow thoughts, when we control our thinking, we control our emotions. She therefore began to affirm: "Divine Presence is in my boss. He loves his wife and children. He laughs with the laughter of God, and Infinite peace floods his mind." Whenever she thought of him, she said:

"God loves and cares for you." She began to cleanse her own mind and took the first step in establishing a harmonious relationship with him. She saw that he's an expression of the Infinite and has the same mind as she has, for there's only one mind common to all individuals.

She constantly affirmed: "I steadfastly refuse to take note of anything less than the Presence of God in my employer. Spirit is closer than my breath and nearer than my hands and feet." In claiming that God dwelled within him and permeated his entire being, she succeeded in immunizing herself to her previous irritation.

⌐✦¬

If you're suffering from an illness, begin to claim: "God's Healing Presence permeates every atom of my being." The recognition of the Infinite One heals and restores you. It made you from a cell and knows all the processes and functions of your body. It's the miraculous Healing Power. It says: "I am the Lord, your God, Who heals you. I will restore your health and mend your wounds."

God is the Life Principle animating all things. He seeks to express Himself through you as harmony, health, joy, wholeness, beauty, and perfection. Love can't wish for anything unloving or for sickness or death, for that would be a contradiction.

If you swim against the current or against the waves of the sea—getting angry, resentful, or jealous—you're going contrary to the law of life and will get tossed about. Instead, align yourself with the Infinite ocean of love within you. Swim with the tides of truth and beauty.

⌐✦¬

Never entertain rigid beliefs about religion. You also must not claim as true something that modern science has shown to be completely false—such as saying that the end of the world is coming.

In the Bible, the *world* means false beliefs, such as fear, hate, and resentment. It's the mass mind. When you die to all of these negative beliefs, that's the end of your narrow, limited world, but it's not the end of the universe at large.

※✠※

God is the Principle of Infinite Intelligence operating in all people, animals, and things in the entire cosmos. To deny the existence of a Creative Intelligence is a complete contradiction of scientific evolutionary findings. As Dr. Cressie Morrison, former president of The New York Academy of Sciences, writes: "We are still in the dawn of the scientific age, and every increase of light reveals more brightly the handiwork of an Intelligent Creator. We have made stupendous discoveries with the spirit of scientific humility and with our faith grounded in knowledge. We are approaching ever nearer to an awareness of God."

※✠※

Your great-grandfather rode on a donkey or a horse; today you ride in a modern jet. At one time, people communicated with each other by using the pony express, but now you can use the phone or e-mail to reach others instantly—even if they're thousands of miles away. Perhaps you can also communicate telepathically. Likewise, you shouldn't cling to outdated ideas but need to allow your religious understanding to evolve.

What are *your* religious beliefs? Are they of the horse-and-buggy type? Or have you advanced with the information age? Let's enter into the high oscillations of Spirit by focusing our attention on God, the Only Presence and Power. *The light of the body is the eye: if therefore thine eye be single, thy whole body shall be full of light. With mine eyes stayed on thee, there is no evil on my pathway now and forevermore.*

In a Nutshell

Today's scientists can't afford to have a closed mind. New discoveries and revelations are compelling them to discard the old materialistic concepts of the 19th century. They're learning that we're living in an ever-changing, fluid universe and that the entire cosmos is a mental phenomenon.

You must discard old superstitions and false beliefs about an avenging God, hell, purgatory, the devil, and evil forces. Realize that these are simply states of mind created by our ancestors because they were ignorant and didn't understand the laws of the universe.

There's only One Power. When you use It constructively and peacefully, you call It *God, health,* and *happiness.* When you use It ignorantly, stupidly, or maliciously, you call It *evil, Satan, misery, misfortune,* and so on. However, there's but *One* Presence.

Your deep-seated beliefs and emotional espousals govern you. Whatever idea or belief is dominant in your subconscious mind takes control of your thoughts, actions, and reactions. If you believe in failure or think that you're jinxed, you can't succeed. You can work extremely hard for 18 hours every day, but you'll still fail if defeat is the main idea in your mind. What's the preeminent idea that in *your* mind? *According to your belief is it done unto you.*

Raise your sights and strike out for the good life. You can stay in the valley or climb the mountain. Spirit is supreme. It's the Eternal Source of all things.

If you're dwelling on the shortcomings of other people, you're creating problems in your own mind, body, and pocketbook. If you're jealous of another person, you're demeaning and impoverishing yourself. You're putting the other person on a pedestal and saying, "You can have these things, but I can't. You have the power to disturb me." You're thereby denying your own Divinity and affirming lack and limitation.

God is the Life Principle animating all things. It seeks to express Itself through you as harmony, health, peace, joy, wholeness, beauty, and perfection. Love can't wish for anything unloving or for illness or death.

If you swim against the current or against the waves of the sea—getting angry, resentful, or jealous—you're going contrary to the law of life and will get tossed about. Instead, align yourself with the Infinite ocean of love within you. Swim with the tides of truth and beauty.

Chapter Six

Every End Is a Beginning: Life after Death

*W*ill we live again? This question has been asked millions of times. The truth is that there's no death in the sense of oblivion. God is life, and that life is our life now. It has no beginning or end. Since human beings are manifestations of God, we can't die.

We shouldn't think of death as a loss but as a new birthday in God. Instead of having depressing thoughts about departing from the Earth, let's think about reuniting with all of our loved ones and arriving at our new destination.

Spirit was never born and will never die. When our body no longer serves us, it's cast aside. Spirit then clothes Itself in a new body. As Emerson wrote: "Every spirit builds itself a house . . ." We have bodies to infinity, and we'll never be without one. The fourth-dimensional body is rarified but is nevertheless a body.

⊨✠⊨

We seem to be struck numb with fear at the thought of dying. But we shouldn't be afraid of the end of this existence because it's simply giving up the old for the new. Death and birth are two sides of the shield of life. When we pass on to the next dimension, we'll have full use of our mental faculties. We'll recognize our new environment and other souls, and we'll also be known. We'll understand and be understood and advance in all aspects of our being.

⊶✦⊷

When we taste the reality of what we call "death," we'll become aware that it's a new birth, for every end is a beginning. As the great poet John Milton said, death is the golden key that opens the palace of eternity. It's impossible that anything so universal as death could ever be looked upon as evil. The journey is from glory to glory—onward, upward, and godward. We see this process every spring when the seeds frozen in the ground are resurrected and the desert rejoices and blossoms like a rose.

⊶✦⊷

The entry into the next dimension of life is characterized by newness, freedom, and expression. Life is endless expansion. In the next phase of being, you'll possess a memory of life on this earthly plane and know who and what you are. You'll have a link that reminds you of the continuity of your individual life as you keep on expanding without cease. God is Infinite, and so are you. Never in eternity could you exhaust the glories, beauties, and wonders that are in you. That's how amazing you are.

⊶✦⊷

Every baby is born with universal life, for the Divine assumes the form of all infants. Birth is really God coming down from heaven and appearing in an earthly body. Therefore, we all contain the Presence and Power in our subconscious. When our physical body ceases to function, we put on a fourth-dimensional body, frequently referred to as the *subtle, celestial, astral,* or *subjective body.* The only thing we take with us to the next phase of life is our state of consciousness, our faith, and our knowledge of God's eternal laws.

⌖

When I was asked to conduct a meditation at the home of two young women whose father had recently died, one of the daughters said, "I know Dad is alive with the life of God and that he's functioning at a higher frequency. We want to pray for him and radiate love to him, which will aid him on his continuing path."

Her sister added, "Our father's life here on this plane has ended and a new life has started."

The daughters knew that every end is a beginning. As we have borne the image of the earthly, we shall also bear the image of the heavenly. In other words, someday we'll shed this physical self and go to the next dimension. We don't take it with us when we enter the higher oscillations of Spirit where our bodies become rarefied.

⌖

When you came into this world, you were received by loving hands. You were coddled and adored, and all of your needs were met until you grew out of childhood. What's true on one plane is true on all planes, for God is love. When you enter the next dimension, you'll meet all of your loved ones again and have a happy reunion. You'll do many of the things you enjoyed in this life and many that you never had the opportunity to try before, but you'll be operating on a new wavelength, at a higher frequency. You'll find a counterpart of everything in this world in the next plane, for as in heaven, so on Earth.

⊷✛⊶

A woman who'd lost two sons in the Korean War—one 19 years old and the other 20—told me that the news of their deaths was agonizing at first. She said that she soon regained inner peace, however, by quietly affirming to herself: "He is not a God of the dead, but a God of the living, for all live unto Him."

She looked at me with a rare radiance in her eyes as she said, "Do you know what I experienced?" Her words came slowly and with majestic calm: "Suddenly I felt a wave of serenity come into my heart, and all sense of grief disappeared. I knew and felt that they were alive, and I could sense their presence and kind touch. It was a wonderful experience. I know that God is just and good, and I realize that while I miss them, they're now building another home for themselves in the next dimension of life, where they have new bodies and tasks to accomplish."

The woman continued, "I asked myself, *How can I help them?* The answer came quickly: *Pray for them.*" So she prayed as follows:

> *My sons were loaned to me by God, the Source of all life and the Giver of all gifts. I knew that I could not have my boys forever and that one day they would leave me, get married, and perhaps move to another city or go to a foreign land. I loved them while they were with me. I gave them everything I could in the way of love, faith, confidence, and trust in God. My mission now is to help them build a new home. I radiate love, peace, and joy to them. God's light and truth flow through them. His peace fills their souls. I rejoice in their journey, for life is progression. Whenever I think of my boys, I say, "God is with them and all is well."*

This prayer, which she repeated several times a day for a few weeks, brought her a complete sense of well-being and tranquility.

We must teach everyone that they should never grieve or mourn for loved ones. By radiating the qualities of love, peace, and joy to those who have gone to the next dimension, we're lifting them up in consciousness, knowing that the Presence of God is where they are—and where God is, there can be no evil.

In order to pray for the so-called dead, we must affirm that our dear ones who have passed on are now dwelling in a state of bliss rather than lamenting that they're dead or gone. Then we're raising them up because they can feel our prayers and are thereby blessed. Let's see them living in a state of indescribable beauty.

⁂

President Kennedy and Martin Luther King aren't buried anywhere, and neither is anyone else because nobody dies. If someone is lost at sea, do you put a cross where he went down and say, "This is where he died"? Of course you don't, for life has no beginning and no end. In fact, all graveyards tell lies—as you know very well. The tombstones are inscribed: "He died in 1991" or something of that nature, but they're not true at all. In fact, we should never visit cemeteries because no one is there. As Tennyson wrote: "Thou wilt not leave us in the dust: Thou madest man, he knows not why; He thinks he was not made to die; And thou hast made him: thou art just."

⁂

A friend of mine was weeping over a grave. I explained to him, "Your wife isn't there; she's in the next dimension of life where you go every night when you sleep. The earthly body undergoes the natural process of dissolution and becomes grass, trees, and hills; but she has put on a new fourth-dimensional body."

I explained to him, "You're identifying with endings and limitation and are building a cemetery of grief and sorrow in your own mind, which brings all manner of disease into your life. That certainly isn't helping your wife. She's alive with the life of God and would want you to bless her and realize that love, peace, and harmony are flowing through her."

He saw the point and stopped feeling desolate. After all, why should we identify with finality and death when life has no beginning or end? Instead, we need to offer the flowers of our heart and exalt those who have passed on. We need to see them as happy and free and realize that God's presence is within them. We should realize that the joy of the Lord is their strength and that they're illumined and inspired. They're moving through the currents of eternity.

It's impossible to bless your loved ones and feel sorrow at the same time. Therefore, stop building a graveyard in your mind. No one is buried anywhere, and there shouldn't be any monuments to death. Instead, exalt faith, love, and joy.

⊨✟⊨

When faced with loss and tragedy, you can rise above it. Come out of your hole of grief by focusing on the qualities of love, friendship, and faith. Concentrate on your desire to give your talents to the world. As you do so, even though you may still experience loneliness and sorrow, you're building another house in your mind in which you'll dwell shortly if you maintain your trust in the One Who Forever Is. He won't let you down, for He never fails. Endure your present trouble while praying for the great joy that's set before you.

⊨✟⊨

I've been at the bedside of many men and women during their transition and have never seen any of them show any signs of fear. They intuitively know that they're entering into a larger dimension of life. Although we all have a natural wistfulness about our loved ones after they leave this earthly plane, we must realize that they're now living in another mansion of our Father's house and that they're separated from us only by a higher frequency.

The so-called dead are all around us—we just can't all perceive them. It's just like a radio. When you turn the dial, you can hear the President speaking or listen to a song or story. The sounds are already in the air, but you need to tune in to the correct frequency to hear them. If you have clairvoyant or clairaudient ability, you can become aware of the spirits around you who are alive with the life of God. When the scales of false belief fall from your eyes, you'll realize that you have an existence beyond time and space. You'll see and feel the presence of those whom you now call "dead."

⊶✦⊷

Many years ago, I became quite ill and was unconscious for about three days. All this time, I was outside my body and talked with relatives long since gone from the face of the earth—I recognized them clearly. I knew I had a body, but it was a different one with powers that enabled me to go through closed doors. Everything seemed to be alive. Whenever I thought of a place—such as London, Paris, or Belgium—I was transported there instantaneously. I could see and hear everything that was going on. I spoke to friends and loved ones in the next dimension of life. Everyone there communicated solely through thought, rather than speech. I had no sense of time and felt free and ecstatic.

I saw the doctor come into the room where my body was lying and heard him say, "He's dead." I felt him touching my eyes and testing my responses. I tried to tell him that I was alive, but he didn't seem to know I was there. I touched him and said, "Leave me alone. I don't want to come back." However, he didn't seem to feel or hear me.

Then the physician gave me an injection that seemed to be a heart stimulant of some kind. I was upset because I didn't want to come back. It was so beautiful in the transcendent state and I was just beginning to enjoy myself and to know my new acquaintances and studies in the next dimension. However, I was being restored to earthly life, and I felt myself going back into my body. Suddenly everything seemed to pass away and I felt like I was in prison. When I awakened, I was suffering from shock, undoubtedly due to the anger expressed in the fourth-dimensional body before it entered into its three-dimensional counterpart.

As far as I know, I had an experience of what the world calls *death*. When we're dead, we're actually functioning in a higher dimension of mind.

⊰✛⊱

A brilliant surgeon said to me, "You know, after I operate on people, some of them tell me everything that happened in the operating room and all of the instructions I gave to the nurses while they were under anesthesia." He continued, "I have had that experience time and time again—at least a hundred times in the last 25 years. Patients tell me that they were floating up in the room over the operating table and that they heard everything I said and saw everything I was doing." How true that is!

⊰✛⊱

I visited Dr. Viktor Frankl some years ago. He's a psychiatrist and the author of *Man's Search for Meaning* and many other books. He has a wonderful knowledge of the great laws of mind and the way of the spirit. He told me, "Once an elderly practitioner consulted me because of his severe depression. He couldn't get over the loss of his wife, who'd died two years before and whom he'd loved above all else. Now, how could I help him? What should I say to him? Well, I refrained from telling him anything, but instead asked him a question: 'What would have happened, doctor, if you'd died first and your wife had had to survive you?' 'Oh, he answered, 'that would have been terrible for her. She would have suffered greatly.' Then I said, 'You see, you've spared her that pain, but now you have to pay for it by experiencing your grief for her.' He said no more but shook my hand and calmly left my office."

Dr. Frankl observed that when we can find meaning in our suffering, it ceases to cause us pain. He added, "I couldn't change my patient's fate or bring back his wife, but in that moment, I did succeed in changing his attitude since he could now see a purpose for his agony."

❈

A few years ago, I conducted a funeral for the wife of an old friend of mine. They'd been married for about 45 years, and he said that he was depressed and lonesome. He visited the grave every morning. He couldn't sleep at night and was taking tranquilizers and sedatives. He said that life wasn't worth living and talked about the futility of everything.

I responded as Dr. Frankl had to his patient. I said, "Suppose your wife had passed on first. How would she have felt?"

He answered, "She would have been terribly depressed, and I would never have wanted that."

"Well," I said, "don't you see? You're carrying that burden for her now. You're saving her from that sorrow. And she's alive in the next dimension. Whenever you think of her, claim that she's filled with the life of God. Think of beauty instead of ashes and death. Affirm that the life of God flows through her and that the joy of the Lord is her strength. In Him, there's fullness of joy and no darkness at all."

The man understood. He realized that by getting mired in grief and depression, he wasn't helping her. She was in the next plane, and it's a holy act to pray for those who have passed on so that they may be released from any kind of problem—just like we pray for someone in the hospital. Our affirmations help them.

After we talked, my friend began to radiate love, peace, and goodwill to his beloved wife instead of staying stuck in his dejection. He started to exalt the presence of God in her, realizing that He is eternal. There's no end to our glory. Every time he thought of her, he said: "I praise God in the midst of you. The Healing Presence loves and cares for you." He put a little spiritual iodine on his wound of sorrow and experienced a wonderful, wonderful healing.

⋈✝⋈

We don't have the right to hold our loved ones back. For example, if your daughter went to India or somewhere on an assignment, would you feel sad and depressed? Wouldn't you radiate love and say, "Divine love goes before her to make her path joyous and straight. Wherever she is, Infinite Spirit is there, too. The light of God shines in her." Surely that's love! Come into God's presence singing and offering praise. Be thankful unto Him and bless His name, for the Lord is good. His mercy endures for all generations.

⋈✝⋈

Psychics, clairvoyants, and similarly gifted people frequently speak to me after attending one of my lectures. They tell me that they saw people sitting on the platform while I was speaking. In each instance, they've accurately described some of my teachers and relatives who are now in the next dimension. For example, they've seen Emmet Fox, author of *The Sermon on the Mount,* and have described him to me in detail even though they'd never seen him before or heard him lecture. Some didn't even know that he'd passed on. They've also seen Thomas Troward, the author of several books on mental science. They've accurately described my father, who passed away many years ago, as well as my sister and other relatives and friends. In each case, the people who saw these fourth-dimensional beings on my platform had never met them when they were in their earthly bodies.

Many doctors and other medical professionals also have a great gift of clairvoyance and clairaudience. They can see the contents of the mind as well as of the body and describe pathologies without an x-ray. They don't talk about it lest others think that they're strange, but it's well known that some people have such psychic abilities.

⌗✝⌗

A man told me he was about to invest a lot of money ($100,000) in a business venture in Las Vegas. He had a lawyer check it out, and it looked good from every angle. Then the man's father, who'd passed on several years ago, appeared to him in a dream and said that the deal was shady and that he shouldn't get involved. He said, "If you don't think I'm your father, this is the nickname I used when you were a boy." Then he told his son the nickname.

The man woke up and was absolutely convinced that his dad had come to him in his dream. It could well be. At any rate, his mind had given him an answer. He'd prayed for guidance and right action, and that's why the solution came to him. He didn't go through with the deal, and he subsequently discovered that it was an absolute fraud. He would have lost all of his money if he'd invested in it.

⌗✝⌗

Recently I visited a man named John, who was dying of cancer. He'd been sick for two years and had never gone to a doctor or sought aid of any kind because he said he was praying about it. Unfortunately, he didn't even know what prayer really was. He was a good man but had peculiar religious beliefs.

His mind was clear and he wasn't under sedation, but he began to talk to his father and mother who had left this world many years ago. He said, "They're here, and I'm going with them." Then he added, "I see my son, Doug . . . I didn't know that he was in the next dimension." John's wife, who was present at her husband's bedside as he passed on, didn't know about her son's death, either. However, one week later, she received a letter from India, where Doug had been stationed. It turned out that he'd made his transition at about the same time as my visit to his father.

Yes, your loved ones who have passed on are all around you, separated only by frequency. However, your physical eyes are blind to the great invisible reality that surrounds you. You'd see a different world if you began to look through your inner eye of clairvoyance and spiritual perception.

⌖

Fenwick Holmes was over 90 when he passed on, but he was still leading an active life writing and lecturing. He said, "Tell Murphy that I'm going on to the next dimension, which I've seen many times. And let him know that I'm going to work for him there."

Yes, he'd been in the next dimension many times in meditation. As I've written before, you go to that fourth dimension every night when you sleep. As Wordsworth wrote: "Our birth is but a sleep and a forgetting: The soul that rises with us, our life's star, Hath had elsewhere its setting, And cometh from afar. Not in entire forgetfulness, And not in utter nakedness, But trailing clouds of glory, do we come From God, who is our home."

⊯⊹⊨

Our spirit was never born and will never cease to be. The human spirit is birthless, deathless, and changeless. Death can't touch it at all. Our transition from this dimension to another is like taking off our worn-out robes, and replacing them with new ones. As Browning wrote: "All that is, at all, Lasts ever past recall; Earth changes, but thy soul and God stand sure: What entered into thee, *that* was, is, and shall be: Time's wheel runs back or stops: Potter and clay endure."

In a Nutshell

There's no death in the sense of oblivion. God is life, and that life is our life now. It has no beginning or end. Since human beings are God in manifestation, we can't die.

You'll still be you in the next dimension. The only difference is that you'll be operating on a new wavelength at a higher frequency. The Eternal One is within you.

We must teach everyone that they should never grieve or mourn for loved ones. By radiating the qualities of love, peace, and joy to those who have passed over to the next dimension, we're praying for them in the right manner. We rejoice in their new birthday, knowing that the Presence of God is where they are—and where God is, there can be no evil.

In order to pray for the so-called dead, we must realize that the loved ones who have passed on are dwelling in a state of beauty, joy, and love. Then we're lifting them up because they feel our prayers and are thereby blessed. We make them happy with our sincere thoughts.

Grief creates all manner of disease. Furthermore, protracted grief is morbid selfishness. It means that you're only thinking of yourself rather than of your loved one. If you love people who have passed on, you should exalt them and see them as happy and free. Realize that God's presence is within them and that the joy of the Lord is their strength. They're illumined and inspired and are moving through the currents of eternity.

Look upon death as a birth into the fourth dimension. Death can't actually exist because that would be a contradiction. God is life, and how could life die? Life just *is*. We're living in the fourth dimension now. Actually, we're living in all dimensions because we're living in God, Who is Infinite.

Our spirit was never born and will never cease to be. The human spirit is birthless, deathless, and changeless. Death can't touch it at all. Our transition from this dimension to the next is like taking off our worn-out robes and replacing them with new ones.

Chapter Seven

————•❖•————

The Two Worlds You Live In

$\mathcal{W}$e're living in two worlds: the outer, objective world of the senses and the inner, subjective world of thought, feeling, and imagery. To understand the two spheres that each of us inhabits, we have to have wisdom, which means being aware of the Presence and Power of God within ourselves. We need to know that thoughts are things and that whatever we impress in our subconscious mind is expressed on the screen of space—whether it's negative or positive. We become enlightened when we know that we can take any idea and weave it into the fabric of our mind by nourishing it and affirming its reality.

❖

If you identify yourself with negative thoughts and imagery, you can't transform your emotional life. If you attach the words *I am* to unpleasant states by making statements such as "I'm poor," "I'm sick," or "I'm depressed," you can't separate yourself from these negative conditions. You should instead make it a practice to refuse to attach your *I am* to dark emotions and thoughts. Avoid the muddy roads in your mind where fear, resentment, hostility, and ill will lurk. Refuse to listen to discouraging remarks, and don't let dreary moods touch you. Practice inner separation by gaining a new understanding of who you really are.

Begin to realize that you're the Infinite Spirit that lies stretched in smiling repose. Identify yourself with the qualities, attributes, and potencies of the Eternal One; and your entire life will be transformed.

⊶✞⊷

The secret to transforming a negative emotional nature is to practice self-observation and direct your attention inward. This is different from external observation. You may spend a lifetime studying the atoms, the stars, and the world of phenomena, but this can't bring about inner change. You should instead learn to be discerning and separate the chaff from the wheat. Begin by asking yourself: *Is this idea true? Will it bless, heal, and inspire me? Will it give me peace of mind and contribute to the well-being of humanity?*

You can begin to change your inner world through the purification of your thoughts and emotions. Since feelings follow thoughts, if you want to channel your emotions constructively, you need to focus your thoughts on whatever is true, good, lovely, and just.

⊶✞⊷

Do you find yourself reacting in automatic, self-sabotoging ways? Never permit your life to be a series of negative reactions to what you experience every day. Regardless of what happens, your thoughts and feelings should remain fixed on the great truth of the Living Spirit. It's the Life Principle that animates and sustains you and takes care of you when you're sound asleep. It was never born and will never die. Water can't wet It, fire can't burn It, and wind can't blow It away. It's the Eternal Being within you. As you dwell upon this Indwelling Presence and the truths of God, all of your dark thoughts and emotions will be transformed.

❖✝❖

You may be inclined to blame or judge other people because of the way they talk or act. But if what they say or do makes you angry or unhappy, *you* are the one who's emotionally disturbed. What columnists write in the newspaper won't bother you if you know the laws of mind. Others have the freedom to write what they like, and you have the choice to completely disagree with them. Why should you give a piece of paper with words written on it the power to upset you? If you do so, you're actually distressing yourself with your own thoughts and reactions. You can't afford to be negative like this because it depletes your vitality and robs you of enthusiasm. It also makes you physically and mentally ill.

❖✝❖

Perhaps you tend to compare yourself with others. Do you feel inferior in the presence of a person who seems to be more distinguished than you are? Suppose you're a great pianist. When someone praises another musician, do you feel inferior? If you understand that the Presence of God is within you, you won't have such a reaction. When you feel the Infinite Power that lives in the hearts of everyone, you'll know that comparisons are meaningless.

❖✝❖

I asked a man recently, "Have you noticed your typical reactions to people, newspaper articles, and radio commentators? Have you been observing your behavior?" He replied, "No, I haven't." He was living obliviously and not growing spiritually. However, he began to think about his reactions and admitted that many of the things he read and heard in the media irritated him immensely. He was reacting in an automatic manner and wasn't disciplining himself. It makes no difference whether all of the writers and journalists were wrong and he alone was right, for the negative emotion aroused in him was destructive.

⊶✠⊷

When you say, "I think this," "I resent that," or "I dislike this," which *I* is speaking? Isn't it a different one every moment? One minute you're being critical, and the next, you're speaking tenderly. Take a good look at the thoughts you're consorting with in your mind, which is a city teeming with ideas, opinions, feelings, sensations, and beliefs. Some of the places in your mind are slums and dangerous streets. However, the Divine Presence is also there. You can tune in to It, and It always responds to you. Go down the paths of peace, love, joy, and goodwill. You'll find beautiful lighting and wonderful citizens in the better areas of your mind.

⊶✠⊷

I had an interesting chat with a young man who was studying the laws of mind in France. He said that his procedure was to take "mental photographs" of himself from time to time. He would sit down and think about his negative emotions, thoughts, sensations, and reactions. Then he would say, "These are not of God. They are false. I will go back to the God Presence and think from the standpoint of truth, beauty, and love." He practiced the art of inner separation. He'd stop when he got angry and say, "This is not the Infinite One speaking, thinking, or acting. It's the false thought in me."

Every time you start to get, critical, depressed, or irritable, you can also think of the Divine Presence and love within you. Ask yourself: *What is the nature of God and heaven?* The answer is that everything is bliss, harmony, peace, and joy.

⊶✠⊷

All men and women fundamentally want to be good and express their Divinity. If you've engaged in destructive acts and have robbed and defrauded others, you can rise out of the slum of your mind to that place in your own consciousness where you cease to condemn yourself. The Absolute does not and cannot condemn or punish you. You're your own persecutor and tormentor, and it's foolish to be harsh with yourself. When you cease to accuse yourself, the world will no longer accuse you. This is the power of the Divine Presence within you.

Suppose you've committed criminal acts. It wasn't God within Who did these things; it was the mass mind in you or your conditioning. Perhaps you were brought up with prejudices, fears, and so forth. This hostility and anxiety becomes compulsive, you know, because the nature of the subconscious is compulsive. Of course, this doesn't excuse you from your responsibility. You're in charge of the way you think, feel, and act. You're responsible if you put your hand in the fire and get burned or if you run a red light and get a ticket.

Begin to affirm: "I am strong, illumined, inspired, loving, kind, and harmonious." Whatever words you attach to the *I am* within you, you become. Feel these states of mind and affirm them, and then you'll begin to truly live in the garden of God. The *I am* in you means God, light, awareness, and your true self. It's the only Cause and Power in the world. Honor It and realize that the Living Presence is within you. The law is: I am that which I feel myself to be.

A you continue to say to claim: "I am strong, illumined, inspired, loving, kind, and harmonious; I am prosperous and inspired from On High," you'll populate the heavens of your mind with God's eternal verities. As the Bible says: "Fear not for I have redeemed you . . . When you pass through the waters, I will be with you; And through the rivers, they shall not overflow you." This is the power within you.

⊯✚⊭

Keep in mind that when you pray about anything, it's necessary to meditate on your desire and nourish and sustain it. Gradually, it will sink into your subconscious mind and manifest on the screen of space. A wonderful prayer is: "I am Spirit; I think, feel, see, and live as the Infinite Presence Almighty within me." As you continue to repeat this affirmation, you'll begin to feel a oneness with the Divine. As the sun in the heavens redeems the earth from darkness and gloom, so will the realization of the Presence of God in you reveal the person you always wished to be—a joyous, radiant, peaceful, successful individual illumined from On High.

⊯✚⊭

The external world in which we live is constantly changing. Indeed, the ancient Greek philosopher Heraclitus said that no one steps into the same river twice. You can't step into the same river of mind more than once, either. As you're reading this book, the river of the mind is flowing through you, receiving Divine ideas and constantly evolving. You're not the same person you were 5, 10, or 20 years ago. Every time you develop your spiritual values or have a new insight, you're transformed. Therefore, you may not be the same person you were last week. The cells in your body are dying by the millions, and new ones are taking their place.

Realize that everything is changing, and don't fight it. You must be like the willow tree that bends in the wind rather than becoming rigid and snapping apart in a storm. When you know the truth that God dwells in you, you forever exalt the Divine Presence and are moving onward, upward, and godward. The Eternal One is within you. As the poet Henry Lyte wrote: "Change and decay in all around I see: O Thou who changest not, abide with me!"

⊯✚⊭

The Bible says: "Take your sandals off your feet, for the place where you stand is holy ground." Of course, the scriptures are allegorical, and in this passage, *feet* represent understanding. To *take off your sandals* means to divest yourself of all false ideas, beliefs, opinions, and dogmas and realize once and for all that the Divine Presence is within you. It's the heart of the true temple, which you enter through faith in the Living Presence of God and through love and goodwill for all people. So go into the holy of holies within yourself and realize that the place where you stand is hallowed ground. It has nothing at all to do with the soil. God created the entire world, and *every* place is sacred. God is omnipresent, which means that He's not just in a particular shrine or church but also in the street and marketplace. He's in the abode of sin as well as in the house of prayer. Let go of any false beliefs and realize that God is the Living Spirit within you and that He responds to your thoughts. Experience the joy of an answered prayer.

Thoughts and feelings create your destiny because they're Divine agents. Go into your inner world and realize that you're now what you long to be. Claim it, feel it, believe it, and exalt it . . . and it will come to pass. Yes, take off your sandals and you can change the outer world of conditions, experiences, and events.

⛧

External things aren't causative unless you make them so. There's no power in the weather, for example, and a cool breeze won't give you a cold. You can, of course, argue that a fan will give you a stiff neck or make you ill, but it's actually innocuous. You've just transferred the power within you to the fan, which is simply molecules moving at a high speed. Stop giving your power to the weather, the stars, the sun, and the moon. In addition, don't place any person on a pedestal. If you do so, you're honoring a false god. In fact, you shouldn't worship any being other than the Eternal Presence within you.

❊❖❊

In the United States, we have Republican and Democratic conventions in which each party promulgates a "platform." Well, they're not talking about the piece of wood on which they stand but about the principles they espouse. Similarly, you're also standing on a platform of your faith, convictions, and beliefs. If you believe in failure or have a fear of it, you'll experience defeat because you've put your faith in the wrong thing. But if you have faith that you were born to win, you'll succeed.

In the midst of confusion, maintain your strong conviction that the Divine Presence within you is All-Wise. Realize that one with God is a majority. If He's for you, who can be against you?

❊❖❊

I remember an Englishman who believed that he and his family were cursed. He told me that this curse had followed them down through the generations. I said to him, "Read the 91st Psalm and know that God is guiding you and watching over you and that He always sustains and strengthens you." *Because thou hast made the Lord, which is my refuge, even the most High, thy habitation; There shall no evil befall thee, neither shall any plague come nigh thy dwelling. For he shall give his angels charge over thee, to keep thee in all thy ways. They shall bear thee up in their hands, lest thou dash thy foot against a stone.*

I told him that if he repeatedly affirmed these truths, he would impregnate his subconscious and lead a charmed life. This all happened 40 years ago, and he's alive and well today. He succeeded in neutralizing his negative belief in a family curse.

❊❖❊

If I give you a lecture on sodium chloride and tell you that it's known as *salt,* has been used down through the ages as a preservative, and gives flavor to food, you might say, "That's very interesting." Since you've tasted salt, you know what I'm talking about. However, if I tell you all about pomegranates, which you've never tried, you don't really understand what they are because you've never tasted them. In the same way, you must experience the sweet savor of God for yourself. You must absorb these truths and incorporate them in your subconscious mind, where they become a living part of you. You can give theoretical assent to certain truths and memorize the psalms, but that means nothing unless you believe in your heart that God leads you to green pastures and that goodness and mercy follow you all the days of your life.

As you absorb these truths and let them become part of you, you'll be filled with enthusiasm, energy, and joy. You'll accomplish great things because you'll have so much zeal and inspiration. *Blessed are those who hunger and thirst for righteousness, for they shall be filled.*

⸎

Are you governed by the propaganda of the world and the mass mind? If so, you're a frightfully confused person. You need to develop inner conviction and realize that the Supreme Creative Intelligence is within you. *To believe* is to accept something as true, and whatever you believe comes to pass—whether it's good or bad. What you feel, you attract; and what you imagine, you become. Therefore, if you believe that God is guiding you and that success, abundance, and right action are yours, all of these things will manifest. After all, God didn't give you a spirit of fear; He endowed you with love, peace, and a sound mind. Ask yourself: *Am I directed by the external world or mass mind, or is the inner world of my subconscious in charge of my life?*

⊯✛⊯

Love was never born and will never die. It's within you. When you radiate compassion to your child, you're expressing that Infinite ocean of love. When you lift a table, you're using the One Power that moves the world. And when you solve a problem for a loved one, you're drawing on the Intelligence that animates all things and knows only the answer.

⊯✛⊯

Dr. Lothar Von Blankschmidt is a scientist. He told me that when he has an extremely difficult problem, he stills his mind and says to himself, "Infinite Intelligence knows the answer and reveals it to me now." He says that the solution often arrives when he's preoccupied with something else. He receives many answers in that way.

⊯✛⊯

Charles W. told me that he was terrified because the doctor had told him that a growth on his neck was malignant. He said that he left the office hurriedly and didn't go back for three months. He was living in fear and felt tormented. As a result, he developed high blood pressure and bleeding ulcers and had to go to a hospital. While he was there, the doctor examined the growth on his neck and said, "Let me burn this off—it's just a benign tumor."

Well, here Charles had been living in fear and mental torment for three months, thinking that he had cancer. He refused to face his fear and became his own worst enemy. His anxiety about a false diagnosis caused him to develop an assortment of medical problems.

It's wise to confront your challenges directly rather than avoid them as Charles did. As Dale Carnegie said, "Do the thing you fear to do and keep on doing it . . . that is the quickest and surest way ever yet discovered to conquer fear." It should reassure you to know that all problems and illnesses are Divinely outmatched.

⊷✛⊶

I remember reading about a U.S. Navy officer who was diagnosed with cancer. He said, "Why do people become terrified when they get cancer or even hear that word? I'm going to be healed." And he did achieve a complete remission. He subsequently received thousands of letters asking him how he'd overcome the disease. He explained, "I believed in the Bible, which says: 'I am the Lord that healeth thee.'"

It's simple, isn't it? He wasn't afraid of cancer. After all, the Infinite Intelligence creates everything. Your body is the handiwork of God, and I would insult your intelligence if I told you that the Infinite One that made your body and knows all of its processes and functions can't heal you. *I am the Lord that healeth thee, Who satisfies thy mouth with things, and Who restoreth thy youth. God in the midst of you is healing you now.*

In a Nutshell

We're living in two worlds: the outer, objective world of the senses and the inner, subjective world of thought, feeling, and imagery. To understand the two spheres that each of us inhabit, we have to have wisdom, which means being aware of the Presence and Power of God within ourselves.

You're wise when you know that thoughts are things; what you feel, you attract; and what you imagine, you become. Whatever you impress in your subconscious mind is expressed on the screen of space—whether it's good or bad. Therefore, an enlightened person will focus on whatever is true, noble, and lovely.

Every time you're about to get angry, critical, depressed, or irritable, think of the Divine Presence and love within you. Ask yourself: *What is the nature of God and heaven?* It's bliss, harmony, peace, and joy.

When you pray about anything, it's necessary to meditate on your desire and nourish and sustain it. Gradually, it will sink into your subconscious mind and manifest itself in the external world.

You're forever changing. The cells in your body are dying by the millions, and new ones are taking their place. Don't resist change, for it's inevitable.

Thoughts and feelings create your destiny because they're Divine agents. Therefore, go into your inner world and claim that you're now what you long to be. Feel it, believe it, and exalt it; and it will come to pass.

If you believe in failure or have a fear of it, you'll suffer defeat because you have faith in the wrong thing. But if you believe that you were born to win, you'll succeed.

God didn't give you a spirit of fear; he endowed you with love, peace, and a sound mind. God is the Creative Power within you. If you believe that He is guiding you and that success, abundance, and right action are yours, all of these things will come to pass.

Chapter Eight

The Spiritual Meaning of Marriage and Divorce

*T*he Bible says: "Whosoever shall put away his wife, saving for the cause of fornication, causeth her to commit adultery: and whosoever shall marry her that is divorced committeth adultery." The literal meaning of this passage is obvious, but let's consider it from a symbolic perspective. When you devote yourself to the Living Spirit Almighty, realizing that there's no other power, you "marry" the One Presence. You therefore don't want to espouse fear, doubt, anger, voodoo, or anything of that nature because that would be adultery. You shouldn't give any allegiance to the sun, the moon, the stars, other people, or anything else because you're married to God.

Fornicate in the Bible means mental and emotional intercourse with false ideas. For example, if you give your attention to fear, doubt, anxiety, and self-condemnation, you're cohabiting with evil in the bed of your mind. This is absurd, of course, for God is the Only Presence and Power.

⌖

In prayer, you're marrying an ideal, a goal, or an objective. You realize that you have one purpose and make a decision to focus on it. If you're running a business, you give your attention, loyalty, and devotion to it. You're not going to dwell upon fear, failure, or other negative outcomes. If you turn your attention away from your goal of success or achievement, you aren't being loyal to your ideal and are committing adultery because you're betraying your commitment to God. You're saying, "I can't achieve that; God can't do it for me." On the contrary, with God, *all* things are possible.

⊶✛⊷

For those who aren't spiritually aware, the biblical commandments about marital fidelity may seem like a restraint upon their instincts, passions, and appetites. In fact, they're guidelines that point the way to harmony, health, and peace. They're based upon the great laws of life that are written in your heart. When you find marriage confining and say you want your freedom, it's because you're restricted inside. After all, external realities are just projections of internal states of mind.

⊶✛⊷

True marriage is the holiest of all earthly institutions. It should be entered into reverently, thoughtfully, and with a deep understanding of its spiritual significance. Marriage is an accord of Divine ideas, harmony, and purity of purpose. Peace, love, and honesty must prevail in the mind and heart of both husband and wife. From this inner state of conscious unity, a corresponding outer state of peace and joy develops.

⊶✛⊷

It's not a real marriage if a man marries a woman because of her wealth, social standing, or political connections—or merely because she's young and beautiful and he wishes to exalt his ego.

Actually, that's a sham. Similarly, when a woman marries a man because of his profession, for her own personal security, or for any reason other than love, the marriage is a masquerade. It's not a union of true adoration and Divine understanding.

⇥✝⇤

I've performed marriage ceremonies for men and women of advanced years—sometimes as old as 80 or 85. The fires of sex have died out in many of these cases, but God (meaning love) brings them together for the simple reason that they're sincere and truthful with each other. They seek loving companionship and want to share their joys and experiences. Some of these couples have traveled to many parts of the world after their marriage. When a husband and wife have honesty, sincerity, and love, they have a true marriage no matter how old they are.

⇥✝⇤

If you want to attract the right companion, use the following spiritual approach: First, still your mind. Then think clearly about the attributes you admire—such as spirituality, loyalty, faithfulness, honesty, intelligence, and prosperity. Gradually, these qualities will sink into your subconscious mind. Infinite Intelligence always takes over when you pray this way, and you'll attract the right companion. The man or woman you draw to yourself will be the image and likeness of the ideal on which you meditated. You'll harmonize perfectly and will have mutual love, freedom, and respect. This is a marriage made in heaven, meaning in peace and understanding of the laws of mind.

⇥✝⇤

The question frequently arises: Should I get a divorce? This is an individual problem, and I can't offer general answers. Divorce may be right for one person and wrong for another. However it's more noble and godlike to get divorced than to live a lie. For instance, sometime ago, I talked with Elena, who'd been deceived by her husband. He'd told her before they got married that he was a representative for a New York concern, that he was single, and that he belonged to a church organization—all of which were lies. It turned out that he was an ex-convict and a wife beater and that he was living with another woman when he married Elena. She'd loaned him some money, thereby whetting his taste for more, which is the real reason he married her.

Elena thought that it was a sin to get a divorce, but she longed for freedom and peace of mind. I explained to her that she wasn't really married at all, that such a "union" was simply a sham, and that she was living a lie. She immediately proceeded to dissolve the fraudulent marriage.

⌗✛⌗

When a man says, "I came home one night and my wife was gone; we'd been married for 20 years, and I didn't know that she was unhappy," you can rest assured that his wife had mentally left the marriage months or years ago. Her subconscious was filled with ideas of leaving, and she was finally compelled to go because whatever enters the deeper mind manifests in the external world.

⌗✛⌗

We must remember that just because a man and a woman have a marriage certificate and live in a house, it's not necessarily a real home. Perhaps it's a place of discord and hate. In this case, if the couple has kids, it's better for them to break up such a union than to subject their children to a poisoned atmosphere that may result in mental disorders, crime, and delinquency of all kinds. It's far better for a child to stay with one loving parent than to live with two who hate each other and fight all the time.

Children grow in the image and likeness of the mental, emotional, and spiritual climate of their surroundings. Therefore, you should practice the Presence of God in your home—that's real baptism. You cleanse your mind of all erroneous thoughts and focus on harmony, love, and peace. These qualities sink into the subjective mind of the kids, who grow in grace, beauty, and joy.

※✛※

Many men and women have told me that they feel very guilty about what they call "sex sins." They believe that God hasn't forgiven them. This is absurd. I explain to them that God is the Life Principle and doesn't hold grudges against anyone. They're simply condemning themselves and suffering needlessly as a result. If you burn your finger, you know very well that the Life Principle forgives you by reducing the edema and giving you new tissue and skin. Life holds no grudge against you for hurting yourself and always seeks to heal you. If you've eaten some contaminated meat, Divine Intelligence forgives you by causing you to throw up, thereby cleansing your system of possible food poisoning.

God doesn't judge or punish us. We punish *ourselves* through the misuse of the universal laws and our ignorance, which is the only sin. All of the suffering, crimes, and diseases in the world are caused by this ignorance.

※✛※

In the Bible, Jesus asks a woman caught in adultery: "Woman, where are your accusers? Has no man condemned you?" She answers, "No one, Lord." Then Jesus says, "Neither do I condemn thee. Go now and sin no more." The Divine Spirit can't condemn, and we need to forgive ourselves for harboring negative ideas and committing wrong deeds.

You can transform your life by turning to the Divine Presence within and claiming your freedom and peace of mind. Turn away from the past and completely detach yourself from your former way of living. Mentally and emotionally unite with your aim, which is peace, dignity, happiness, and freedom. As you do so, God in His glory responds at once. You'll find a wave of peace moving through you like the dew of heaven, and the shadows of fear and guilt will pass away. As you cease to judge yourself, you'll find that the world can no longer condemn you.

᛭

I've performed marriage ceremonies for many women who were what the world calls "prostitutes." They chose a new life and married wonderful men. They have children and are respectable. The past is forgotten, and they've become new people in God. They're loyal to their husbands, are wonderful mothers, and have a great reverence for the Divinity that shapes their lives.

᛭

There's nothing evil about sex or anything else that God created and ordained. God commanded, "A man will leave his father and mother and be united with his wife, and they will become one flesh." When you marry, your husband or wife comes first—not your father, mother, sister, or brother. You don't have a marriage at all unless your partner has priority in your life.

In marriage, you give of yourself completely, and sex is an act of love. You know very well that what I'm saying is true. When a couple really cares about each other, they see God in one another, and any children they create together must be born of love. That's an immaculate conception. Their kids are beautiful in every way because they're the gift of love.

❊❊❊

Sex between marriage partners is about the genuine expression of love. However, many men and women have a negative attitude toward it. Some think that it's evil, nasty, and ugly—possibly due to their upbringing or some sexual shock in childhood. Perhaps a mother has said to her daughter, "Men are beasts, and sex is evil," or "All men want only one thing." As a result, the girl grows up thinking that sex is evil, and she becomes frigid. On the contrary, sex is ordained by God and is an act of love.

❊❊❊

A man once told me that before having sex, he and his wife prayed because he viewed intercourse as sinful and unclean. He thought that through prayer, he could exorcise any evil connected with the act. In short, he had contempt for sex and was impotent. He said, "I love my wife spiritually but not physically." He'd separated sexual love from spiritual love, which was a stupid and hypocritical thing to do.

I explained to him that marriage is a total union of body and soul. *A man shall cleave unto his wife and they shall be one flesh.* He thereafter began to affirm: "I love my wife spiritually, mentally, emotionally, and physically. She is God's child; and I radiate love, peace, and goodwill to her. God's love flows from me to her; and our sexual relationship is joyous, loving, and harmonious. We share love, freedom, and respect."

After a few weeks, his impotence disappeared, and he enjoyed a harmonious union with his wife. He intuitively perceived a great truth: God gave him the desire to attract a woman and gave his wife the desire to attract a man.

❊❊❊

Susan L. came to see me when she was about to get her fifth divorce. She was exceedingly bitter and resentful toward her present husband—as well as toward all the previous ones. She'd remarried each time without forgiving and mentally releasing her ex-husbands, and each was worse than the preceding one. Her anger had caused her to attract similar types of men because of the law of attraction.

The cure was for Susan to forgive herself and all her former husbands and to focus her mind on the kind of man she desired. We draw people to us who have qualities that are like our own. When we discipline our mind in prayer and enter into the spirit of forgiveness, we can attract individuals with higher spiritual qualities.

⊶✝⊷

If a man has love and respect for his wife, he won't want any other woman. When he's found his true spiritual ideal in marriage, he doesn't seek love in the arms of another. On the other hand, a man who runs around with many women probably has a sense of inadequacy. He's trying to prove his masculinity because he's really sick inside and is wedded to frustration, resentment, and cynicism. The philanderer has a profound inferiority complex and feels insecure. Furthermore, all the women he meets are neurotic and confused like he is. He's seeing and hearing his own vibrations because birds of a feather flock together.

Let's also take the case of a woman who runs around with a married man. She's been unable to demonstrate a husband or boyfriend, and she gets a false sense of satisfaction or a thrill from stealing another woman's husband. She also has an inferiority complex and is unstable and neurotic.

Instead of falling victim to this kind of insecurity, realize that God in the midst of you is love. Let Him unite you and your partner now. When you've found love with your mate, you will have discovered the fullness of life.

╪

You may ask: Why did some men have many wives in the past? The reason was that at one time, the world was underpopulated, and the earthly fathers, not knowing anything better, engaged in polygamy in order to have many children. Today we're more spiritually awakened and know that the population is big enough.

╪

Sex is part of all life. It's the Infinite Intelligence seeking expression in all its varied forms. Whenever you meditate on the truths of the Divine—or upon any idea—and enter into the feeling of it, that's also an aspect of sex. Prayer is a sexual act because you mentally, emotionally, and spiritually unite with an ideal. Whatever you impress on your subconscious mind is expressed in the external world.

╪

A man once boasted to me that he hadn't had sexual relations with his wife for more than four years because he'd become more "spiritual." He belonged to a strange cult whose leader had told him that in order to advance spiritually, he had to lead an ascetic life and refrain from all intercourse with his wife. This man was neurotic, afflicted with ulcers, and mentally disturbed. He'd been brainwashed into believing that sex was evil and would inhibit his spiritual illumination.

I explained to him that this belief was pure balderdash and was based upon ignorance, superstition, and fear. At my suggestion, he renewed normal relations with his wife, looking upon the act as one of love. He realized that God put him in the world to enjoy all of his senses and to go forth and multiply.

Thereafter, his constant prayer was: "We have a happy, joyous marriage and true and lasting love. Divine love reigns supreme in our marriage now." The couple has become much happier than ever before.

⊰✢⊱

If love is lacking in your life, use this prayer frequently: "God's love, wisdom, and harmony are being expressed through me now. Poise, balance, and equilibrium reign supreme in my life."

As you make a habit of repeating this affirmation, wonders will unfold in your life. Love, inspiration, and guidance will well up spontaneously. You'll become an irresistible magnet and will attract all of the blessings of life from every direction.

⊰✢⊱

Young men and women often ask me if they should experiment with sex before they get married. I tell them that marriage doesn't change anything and that if they freely indulge before marriage, they can't expect fidelity or trust afterward. In addition, they may suffer from life-changing consequences. For example, a young man who was studying physics in New York believed in free love. He had no standards and was having sexual relationships with several women who attended the same college. One became pregnant, and they had a shotgun wedding. He had to quit college and work as a waiter in order to take care of his wife. He'd married a woman he didn't love, and they had a baby neither wanted. Where was his freedom and free love now? He'd placed himself in a prison of lack, resentment, and poverty.

⊰✢⊱

Premarital sexual experiences aren't conducive to a happy married life. Often the man distrusts a woman he can have so easily. He says to himself: *If she will do this before marriage, she will do it with others afterward.* I asked a young man, "Is your girlfriend nobler, sweeter, and more dignified in your eyes now than before you had sexual relations?" He blushed and answered, "No . . . I guess you're right." Happiness in marriage depends upon love, loyalty, honesty, devotion to the truth; and a desire to uplift each other spiritually, mentally, and in all ways. Love doesn't take a woman to a shabby hotel, and we can't experience Divine adoration during an illicit interlude.

⊶✝⊷

To maintain a happy married life, pray with your partner. Affirm frequently: "Divine love, harmony, peace, and perfect understanding are now operating and expressed in our heavenly marriage." Salute the Divinity in each other every morning, noon, and night. Then you'll find that your path is pleasant and peaceful.

⊶✝⊷

I spoke to a woman sometime ago who told me that her husband showered her with gifts and brought toys home to their two children almost every night. Yet he was irritable, cursed at his kids, and snapped at her about the most minor things. In talking to the husband, I discovered that he wanted to be "free," as he called it, and avoid the responsibilities of marriage and fatherhood. Furthermore, he had a deep-seated guilt complex because he was having an affair with another woman and paying all the expenses for her apartment and clothes. The presents that he brought to his family every night were his way of compensating for his guilty feelings and the hostility he felt toward them. He had high blood pressure and stomach ulcers that undoubtedly were due to his feelings of shame and self-condemnation over his illicit behavior.

The husband was open and receptive to the explanation that I offered, and he began to realize that he needed to do some mental work immediately. He had to give up his resentment, hostility, and ill will and build a more harmonious and peaceful existence. He cut off relations with the other woman and began to pray along these lines several times a day:

> *Infinite Intelligence rules and guides me; and I radiate love, peace, and goodwill to my wife and children. I surround them with the circle of God's love, knowing and believing that His compassion, peace, and joy fill their minds and hearts. I forgive myself, and I feel free. I mean this. I am sincere. I know the peace of the Infinite reigns supreme in my home, in my heart and in my family.*

By practicing the laws of mind, he replaced his inner turmoil with peace and goodwill. His new attitude dissolved his physical ailments and brought calm to his troubled mind. He and his wife prayed together every night, and love now rules his home life.

⊨✠⊨

A husband told me that he was being sued for divorce because a Ouija board had indicated to his wife that he was being unfaithful to her. At my request, she came to see me. I explained to her in detail that it was her own subconscious that was generating suspicion and resentment toward her husband. She began to see clearly that her deeper mind had worked through the imperceptible movement of her fingers to cause the Ouija board to give a negative report of her husband. In other words, she was simply talking to herself.

The woman was honest enough with herself to see her error, and she realized that her subconscious was talking back to her, revealing her own suspicions. Both the husband and wife agreed to send thoughts of love, peace, and kindness to one another. This dissolved the negative attitude and brought harmony where discord had reigned. The explanation was the cure.

❧✠❧

A woman was about to break up her home because she believed that her husband no longer loved her. She wanted a house in the country, but he preferred to live in an apartment. They couldn't agree. She told him that he didn't care about her because he wouldn't buy a house. She also told me that she knew that he didn't love her anymore because he smoked constantly even though he knew that she was allergic to cigarette smoke.

In this instance, the woman was certainly emotionally and spiritually immature. The reason she nagged her husband was because she wished to change his habits and make him feel guilty for going against her desires and wishes. I asked to talk to him, and I found that he was deeply resentful. He had a guilt complex and responded to his wife by making cutting, angry remarks over trivial and inconsequential things.

In my presence, they talked about their difficulties, resentments, and hostilities and learned to look at the facts. Each one looked at the situation objectively, and they agreed that they'd been childish. They also realized that by calmly discussing their problems in the spirit of love and harmony, they could reach an agreement. She discovered that her asthma wasn't caused by cigarette smoke but by the deep-seated hatred embedded in her subconscious mind. The fact is that any mental and emotional disturbance may affect the organs and the functioning of the body. Her asthma disappeared shortly after harmonious relations with her husband were established.

They've become a happy couple through the elimination of grudges and emotional blackmail. The wife said, "We tossed a coin about the house in the country. My husband lost, but he's a good sport and loves our new home."

This story illustrates that it never pays to try to coerce someone into giving you your way by subtly trying to make him or her feel guilty. Stop practicing emotional blackmail! It never works. How absurd it is to say, "If you loved me, you'd give up smoking"! Resentment is one of the most expensive things in the world—it robs you of peace, health, vitality, and a sound mind, leaving you a mental and physical wreck. If you indulge in grudges over a long period of time, you'll become cold and callous and begin to hate everyone.

⊭✛⊬

Recently a teacher said to me, "I've had three husbands; and all three have been passive, submissive, and dependent on me to make all the decisions. Why did I attract them?" I asked her whether she'd known that her first husband was a submissive type, and she replied, "Of course not! Had I known, I wouldn't have married him."

Apparently, she hadn't learned anything from the first mistake. The trouble was with her own personality. She was very domineering, and unconsciously wanted someone who would be passive so that she could play the dominant role in the home. This was her unconscious motivation, and her subconscious attracted to her what she wanted. She had to learn to break the pattern by adopting the right prayer process. She began to affirm as follows:

I am building into my mentality the type of man I deeply desire. The husband I attract is strong, powerful, loving, harmonious, and kind. He is spiritually minded, very masculine, successful, honest, loyal, and faithful. He finds love and happiness with me. I love to follow where he leads. He wants me, and I want him. I have these qualities to offer a man: I am honest, sincere, loving, and kind. I have wonderful gifts to offer. They are peace, goodwill, a joyous heart, and a healthy body. I am not a nag and I am not abnormally jealous. I can cherish, love, and admire a man. And he offers me love, peace, and harmony, too. The feeling is mutual. I give and I receive. Divine Intelligence knows where this man is, and the deeper wisdom of my subconscious mind is now bringing us together in its own way. We recognize each other immediately. I release this request to the Infinite Intelligence within that knows what I want and how to bring it to pass. I give thanks for the perfect answer.

Now that's prayer. She knew what she was doing and why she was doing it. She prayed in the above manner every morning and night, affirming these truths and knowing that through frequent habituation of the mind, she'd achieve what she sought.

Several months went by, and she had many dates and social engagements—none of which she enjoyed. When she started to doubt and waver, she reminded herself that the Infinite Intelligence was bringing her desire to pass in Its own way and that there was nothing to be concerned about. Her divorce was granted, bringing her a great sense of release and mental freedom. Shortly afterward, she went to work as a receptionist in a doctor's office. She told me that the minute she saw the physician, she knew that he was the man she'd been praying about. Apparently, he knew it, too, because he proposed to her the first week she was in the office. They're now extremely happy.

The doctor wasn't the passive or submissive type but was a mature adult, a former football player, and an outstanding athlete. He was a deeply spiritual man even though he wasn't a member of a particular church. (You know, some of the most godly people don't belong to any organized religion at all.) She got what she wanted because she claimed it mentally until her desire reached the point of saturation. In other words, she mentally and emotionally united with her idea, and it became part of her in the same way that an apple becomes part of the bloodstream.

⊯✛⊯

Of course, it's not just women who seek an ideal mate. Men also often find it difficult to attract a woman with whom they want to spend their lives. Here's a meditation to help in this quest:

I strongly believe that God dwells within me. I am one with God and with all people. God helps me attract the right woman who is in complete accord with me—a woman with whom I blend spiritually. I know that I can give her love and make her life full, complete, and wonderful. With God's help, I am united with a woman who is spiritual, happy, faithful, and true. She is my ideal companion.

Say this prayer each day and night, and the right woman will be attracted to you.

❈

Prayer heals the wounds of married life. If one of the parties gets angry, resentful, or peeved, the thing to do is to immediately resolve the problem through harmonious thinking. Bless the mood of love and goodwill and burn up every hostile, critical though in the fire of Divine compassion. If a couple does this regularly, their marriage will grow in beauty and love as the years roll by. On the other hand, when the husband or wife focuses on evil or destructive thoughts about their partner, they've deserted God and are an adulterer and fornicator. They'll become morose and hateful; and the end result will be separation, divorce, or annulment of the marriage ties.

❈

I had a rather strange experience one time in Texas. A woman and a man came to see me for counseling in a hotel in Dallas. They said that when they were married, they'd quarreled over a piece of property. They became angry at each other and had gotten divorced. They'd both remarried but said that it was a great mistake because they'd done so on the rebound. They said, "We love each other. What shall we do?" I told them to dissolve the sham of their present marriages, which, of course, were not real unions at all.

They did this and went back to each other. They were humble, admitting their mistake of foolish pride. The Divine Presence brought them together in the first place, and It led them back to the altar of love, which heals and solves all problems.

✢

Occasionally a woman says to me, "I'm in love with a man, but I can't marry him because he's Jewish [or Catholic or a nonbeliever]." That's an absurd statement because love knows no creed or religion. In Him, there are no Greeks or Jews, no males or females, and no now or then . . . there's only the eternal reality flowing on forever. God is impersonal and knows nothing about Christianity, Judaism, or any other "ism." Love transcends all these things because it's Divine. Let love guide your married life, and the peace of God will reign supreme in your home.

✢

Some years ago, I counseled a young lady who'd married a Catholic man. They were deeply in love, but her father belonged to another church and hated Catholics. He told his daughter that he would put a curse on her to dissolve the union.

I explained to her that her dad had no power whatsoever to do what he was threatening and that he was just ignorant. The only power is the Infinite God Presence. It moves as unity and harmony. I said, "Your father has no more ability to hurt your marriage than an old rabbit's foot or a stone in a field."

She began to realize that the only power was in her own thoughts and consciousness—in the Life Presence. It is Omnipotent, and nothing can oppose It. She began to affirm that God had united her and her husband in the first place and that His love surrounded and enfolded them. She claimed that the great peace, beauty, and love of God governed their lives and ruled their hearts. She knew that nothing could come between her and the man she loved.

The sequel to this was that her father killed himself a few weeks later. Hatred kills—it destroys peace, harmony, and the Life Principle within you. And, of course, that's suicide.

⊨✝⊨

If a man loves a woman, he can't do anything unloving. He asks himself: *How can I contribute to her happiness and peace?* He wants her to be joyous and free. Similarly, if a woman loves a man, she exalts God in the midst of him and realizes that God's peace fills his soul and that he's Divinely guided. She affirms that he was born to win and is inspired from On High. As she prays this way, wonders unfold.

⊨✝⊨

To maintain a happy married life, pray with your partner. In addition, never hold on to irritations or disappointments from one day to the next, and be sure to forgive each other for any sharpness before you go to bed. As you go to sleep, let your prayer be: "I sleep in peace, I wake in joy, I live in God, and God lives in me."

The moment you awaken in the morning, claim that Divine Intelligence is guiding you in all ways. Send out loving thoughts of peace and harmony to each other, and think of God and His love. Say quietly, "Thank you, Father, for all of the blessings of the day."

The contemplation of Divine ideals, the study of the mysteries of life, a common purpose, and personal freedom bring about wedded bliss. Be faithful to the great eternal truths of God, which are the same yesterday, today, and forever.

In a Nutshell

If you fill your mind with false beliefs, you're committing adultery in the biblical sense. If you imagine loss and ruminate on ill will and bitterness toward others, you're cohabiting with evil in the bed of your mind.

Whatever you mentally and emotionally unite with in your mind is a marriage. You therefore marry many ideas, beliefs, opinions, dogmas, and creeds.

If you give up on your goal in life and say, "I can't do that," you're claiming that God can't do something. Then you're committing adultery because you're giving your allegiance to a power other than the Divine Intelligence.

Some say that the Bible doesn't allow divorce because it says: "Whosoever shall put away his wife, saving for the cause of fornication, causeth her to commit adultery: and whosoever shall marry her that is divorced committeth adultery." In fact, this passage is symbolic. *Fornication* means cohabiting with grudges, peeves, ill will, bitterness, criticism, or resentment. Doing so is a sign that you're already divorced in your mind because you're separated from harmony, peace, love, and everything that's lovely, noble, and godlike.

Children grow in the image and likeness of the mental, emotional, and spiritual climate of their surroundings. Therefore, practice the Presence of God in your home. Cleanse your mind of all erroneous thoughts and focus on harmony, love, and peace. These qualities will enter into the subjective mind of your kids; and they'll grow in grace, beauty, and joy.

If love is lacking in your life, use this prayer frequently: "God's love, wisdom, and harmony are being expressed through me now. Poise, balance, and equilibrium reign supreme in my life."

As you repeat this affirmation, wonders will unfold in your life. Love, inspiration, and guidance will well up spontaneously. You'll become an irresistible magnet and attract all of the blessings of life from every direction.

If you pray with your spouse every night, you'll stay together. Never hold on to irritations or disappointments, and be sure to forgive each other for any sharpness before you go to bed. The moment you awaken in the morning, claim that Divine Intelligence is guiding you in every way. Send out loving thoughts of peace and harmony and think of God and His love. Say, "Thank you, Father, for all the blessings of the day."

Chapter Nine

Mental and Spiritual Laws
in Light of Emerson (Part I)

Ralph Waldo Emerson was one of the greatest American thinkers. He was born in Boston in 1803 and was the son of a Unitarian minister. Emerson also became a Unitarian minister but resigned from his position in 1832. He belonged to a group of transcendentalists that included Bronson Alcott, Henry David Thoreau, William Ellery Channing, and a number of others.

In Emerson's time, most preachers were talking about sinners in the hands of an angry God. They focused on human wickedness and alienation from the Lord. Emerson, on the other hand, said that such ideas were nonsense and taught that God indwells all people. He called this God Presence the *Over-Soul* and stated that the entire world is simply the Divine Spirit made manifest. He wrote:

> Man is a stream whose source is hidden. Always our being is descending into us from we know not whence. The most exact calculator has no prescience that somewhat incalculable may not baulk the very next moment. I am constrained every moment to acknowledge a higher origin for events than the will I call mine.

The Divine Presence walks and talks in us. Since It is present every-where, It must work through each of us. As the Bible says: "Hear, O Israel: The Lord our God is one Lord."

⊞✦⊞

We're all dependent upon the Life Principle. When we lift a chair, it's the Unseen Power lifting it. The God within watches over us when we're sound asleep, and He controls all of our vital organs. Given that the Infinite Spirit is always observing us, some people are puzzled about why we do things we shouldn't. The answer is that we act against our better judgment because our subconscious assumptions, beliefs, and convictions dictate and control all of our conscious actions.

⊞✦⊞

No one can eat an apple for you—you must do it yourself. If I asked you, "What does the apple taste like?" how could you describe it? In the same way, no one can teach you how to meditate or enter into the silence . . . you also need to do that on your own. You can contemplate God's love quietly in your own soul, leaving behind worldly thoughts and false beliefs. So quiet your mind and turn within to God's Healing Presence. Just imagine that you're in the midst of a great stream and that the Divine Presence is flowing through you as joy, peace, wisdom, and understanding. Say, "God's love fills my soul, and His peace floods my mind."

If you're seeking a healing, turn your thoughts away from the problem or the sickness and dwell upon the Almighty Healing Power of God flowing through you now and restoring your entire being. Hear the doctor congratulate you on the miracle that has happened in your life. You are present with the Lord and will be carried along in the direction of your desire because you're open and receptive to the Holy Spirit within you. *Be still and know that I am God.*

᪻✢᪻

Your thought is creative, so instead of thinking of all the reasons why your desire might not be achieved, say, "God speaks to me through desire. He gave me this wish for beauty, music, healing [or whatever you want]."

The Infinite Presence within you seeks expansion and growth. Therefore, if you're a musician, say, "God flows through me, speaks through me, and plays through me in majestic cadences." You'll bring forth music that stirs the soul. God is indescribable beauty and wants to express this glory through His artists, who are all of us. Therefore, focus on harmony, peace, beauty, and love. Busy your mind with these qualities, and wonders will begin to unfold in your life.

᪻✢᪻

Emerson pointed out that everything in the universe changes and passes away. Nothing is permanent but the soul—the Divine Presence in each of us. The Changeless One is within you now.

᪻✢᪻

If your mind is disturbed and you're mean to yourself, you won't get anywhere in your meditation. If you're dwelling on lack, limitation, and your shortcomings as you're meditating, you'll get very negative results. In true meditation, as Emerson practiced it, you go within, contemplate the truth of God from the highest standpoint, and realize that the Infinite Spirit is pure compassion and can't do anything unloving. You can affirm: "God's love fills my soul, and His peace floods my mind." When God's love enters your soul, you automatically honor the Divinity in everybody.

᪻✢᪻

Emerson had a prophetic mind, and he knew long before the idea became popular that our inner thoughts and feelings slowly weave themselves into our cells and tissues. If we're full of hostility, ill will, and bitterness, then these ugly thoughts express themselves in our body and health. It's therefore wise to shut the door on all ugly thoughts—on your fears and doubts—because the Spirit will honor whatever you claim to be true within yourself. Whatever you impress on your subconscious is expressed, whether it's good or bad.

⌐✝¬

Emerson wrote:

> What we commonly call man, the eating, drinking, planting, counting man, does not, as we know him, represent himself, but misrepresents himself. Him we do not respect, but the soul, whose organ he is, would he let it appear through his action, would make our knees bend. When it breathes through his intellect, it is genius; when it breathes through his will, it is virtue; when it flows through his affection, it is love.

Emerson believed that we're more than machines. In fact, we are God walking the earth. The Divine Presence is infinite, and there's no end to the glory and powers within us. Therefore, open your mind and your heart to let the Holy Spirit flow through you. Relax, let go, and marvelous things will happen in your life.

⌐✝¬

At one point in his life, Emerson suffered from tuberculosis. However, he didn't pray against it, for we're never healed by what we reject but by what we turn to and embrace. Emerson had a kinship with the natural world and was drawn to the beauties and the glories of nature. He realized the oneness of all things and was exhilarated by the Divine Spirit. Naturally, his contemplation of beauty and order transformed his mind, and he experienced a miraculous healing. He cured himself because he contemplated harmony, beauty, love, peace, and the oneness of all things.

※✛※

Everybody knows that honesty is the best policy, but we don't practice it if that truth isn't written in our hearts or incorporated in our souls. We're only giving lip service to the idea. We need to realize, as Emerson pointed out, that when we steal from another, we actually rob ourselves, taking away our own health, happiness, and peace.

When we realize this truth, we stop trying to take advantage of others. We're compelled to be good and honest and to express harmony and beauty because we've incorporated the truth into our being through meditation, prayer, and mystic visioning.

※✛※

Emerson wrote that the mark of intelligence is being able to discern what is true and what is false. The only true ideas are those that heal, bless, inspire, elevate, and dignify our soul. Any thought that instills fear into our mind, demeans us, or is contrary to love and harmony must be false. We need to be able to separate the chaff from the wheat and the false from the real, but sadly, that's a skill that millions of people lack—even students of truth. Many people believe in ideas that are absolutely false, such as fate, luck, and malevolent entities.

※✛※

Many people read books about Science of Mind and philosophy, but they don't assimilate the truth in their soul. If they did, they wouldn't be jockeying for position or trying to push others out of the way, saying that they have to get while the getting is good. They wouldn't be angry because the boss didn't promote them, because they'd realize that we promote ourselves and pay our own salary. Maybe they expected to be passed over because that was their belief or expectation.

You express what you are and can't do otherwise. You may have a beautiful philosophy and lofty ideals, but what you do depends on what you are *inside.* Your subconscious beliefs and convictions dictate and control all of your conscious actions. People who are nasty may want to be nice, but they have unpleasant subconscious beliefs. They go forth with a chip on their shoulder and have an argument before noon. They become incensed even though they know that it's not good for them to be angry. They can't do what they know that should and are only giving lip service to the golden rule.

⊱╬⊰

If we really understood the meaning of the golden rule and followed it, there would be no war, sickness, disease, or crime. We'd need no police, armies, navies, or anything like that. There would be heaven on earth. Unfortunately, most people don't understand the essence of the golden rule. For example, a man goes into a bar and says to the bartender, "The boss is out. Let's have drinks on the house." The customer doesn't know that his own subconscious records his silent motives and that the desire to steal will attract lack and limitation and impoverish him—even if he doesn't end up taking anything. The thought itself is destructive.

Don't take what belongs to another. Infinite Intelligence gave you the desire and will also give you the capacity and the wherewithal to get what you want. You don't have to hurt anyone in this world to fulfill your wishes because you have the unqualified ability to go within and claim your good. The Infinite Spirit will honor your claim and execute it. *Thou art ever with me, and all that I have is Thine. Call upon Him, and He will answer you.*

☒✟☒

A few years ago, a woman told me that she had an appointment with President Kennedy. She was sure that she'd get to see him, but he went on to the next dimension before she could meet him. In fact, the only thing that we can be absolutely sure of is that God is God and that the law is the same yesterday, today, and forever. Everything changes and passes away—including philosophies and religions—but the God Presence is always the same. You can trust that implicitly.

☒✟☒

Emerson wrote: "Look into the eyes of a child and you'll see God there." Talk to the Spirit of your children and claim that God's love, peace, and harmony flow through them. Tell them that they're growing in grace, wisdom, beauty, and understanding. Then the love, light, and glory of God will be resurrected in them.

☒✟☒

If a fortune-teller or a psychic predicts something negative for you, fear may be instilled in your mind; and you'll bring misfortune to pass through your own expectations. Instead, contemplate your good now. Put God back on the throne and realize that what's true of God is true of you. If you think that you're a victim of a malefic configuration of the stars, you've established a new god in your mind—a false diety that's governing and controlling you. The Bible says: "Thou shalt have no other gods before Me." There's only One God, One Presence, and One Power. Nothing can oppose It. As you fill your mind with the truths of the Eternal One, you obliterate anything unlike God in your mind and heart, and your future will be glorious and wonderful.

⚜

Emerson believed that the simplest person who worships God in integrity *becomes* God. This was a controversial thing to say back in the 19th century, but he knew that our welfare is dear in the heart of the Divine Spirit. He argued that we need to get away from false beliefs about a harsh God and realize that Infinite love is within each of us. That's really beautiful. He knew that we can't be separated from harmony, health, peace, friends, love, companionship, or anything else because we're spiritual magnets.

⚜

How many times have you been looking for an answer and discovered just the information you needed when you turned on the television, overheard a conversation, or attended a lecture? Your Higher Self opened up the way for you. How often have you stumbled upon a book that solved your problem? That's the God Presence responding to you in a magnificent, wonderful way. God in the midst of you is mighty to heal, and you're an instrument of the Divine. God needs you where you are; otherwise, you wouldn't be here.

⚜

Emerson said that the soul can't know pain or sickness because it's the Living Spirit Almighty within. It was never born and will never die. Water wets It not, fire burns It not, and wind blows It not away. Only the finite self can be frustrated or hurt. Divine love, sorrow and grief disappear, peace casts out pain, and joy dissolves sadness.

⚜

Emerson believed that the theological concept of original sin was a disease that afflicted the people of his times. "Original sin" is simply forgetting our Divine origins and confusing the commandments of humans for the commandments of God. The "fall of man" is actually the fall of *God;* in other words, when God believes Himself to be human, He limits Himself with His belief in being human. In fact, every child is born with all the powers, qualities, and attributes of God. The resurrection is when we become consciously aware of that fact and call forth the intelligence and the power within us. This knowledge of our Divine origins dissolves all problems.

⊯✢⊯

In Emerson's time (and still today), some people had a weird belief that some individuals are predestined to become murderers, thieves, beggars, and so on. All of this is utter nonsense. We're all volitional beings and fashion our own destiny. Each of us must awaken to the transcendental glory of God within. *Choose ye this day whom ye will serve. I hold before you an open door, which no one can shut.* The Life Principle is God in every person. It's as simple as that.

⊯✢⊯

The greatest of all truths is: "Hear, 0 Israel: The Lord thy God is One Lord." There's only *One* Power. If there were two, there would be chaos and war in the heavens above and the earth beneath. There would be no design or order. If we use the Infinite Power constructively, some call It *God, Brahma* or *Allah.* But if we use the Power ignorantly, they call It the *devil, limitation, misery,* and *sickness.*

In fact, the only absolute evil in the world is the denial of the Presence of God; there's no malevolent entity acting independently. There's only the One Presence and Spirit. If you believe that you've been jinxed or that an evil power is after you, you establish that hypothesis in your mind and invite all manner of trouble into your life. You'll experience the embodiment of your ideas, beliefs, and opinions. If you're afraid that you'll catch a certain disease, then you're turning away from your belief in wholeness, beauty, and perfection. You're permitting that suggestion to enter your mind.

⊯✦⊯

If you think that God is going to punish you, that's your own belief, and you're punishing *yourself.* The Absolute doesn't judge or condemn; instead, It always seeks to heal you. Realize, therefore, that God is love and that His peace fills your soul. The Infinite Intelligence responds to everyone. When you call on Him, He will answer you. He will be with you in times of trouble. God is peace and joy and can't wish you to have pain or sadness. God's will for you is something transcending your fondest dreams.

⊯✦⊯

Emerson believed in the law of parallelism, meaning that whatever you impress on your subconscious mind will come forth as form, function, experience, and event. In other words, "As a man thinketh in his heart, so is he." The heart is your subconscious mind. Therefore, whatever you claim and feel to be true will come to pass—whether it's positive or negative. You become what you contemplate, and nothing happens by chance.

⊯✦⊯

Emerson emphasizes that effortlessness is at the heart of everything. However, many people say, "I must get an answer to my prayer by the 15th of next month," or "I must have $5,000 by Thursday." This is utter nonsense because fear and tension will attract only more lack, delay, suffering, and impediments of all kinds. We need to go back to the Source and realize that God, the Over-Soul, is our everlasting supply. *Great peace have they which love thy law and nothing shall offend them.* And the law is: "I become what I contemplate."

Are you going to say, "It's too hard for me"? *According to your belief, it is done unto you.* As long as you're fighting and straining, you don't accomplish anything or get good results because of the law of reversed effort. Instead, remember the truth that God is always there in times of trouble. Then your mind will become quiet, and the solution will come. That's the wise silence of Emerson. You turn away from the problem and contemplate the Divine Presence within you moving on your behalf. *Call upon Me, and I will answer you.*

❦

Churches have made laws, rules, and regulations; and you can observe all of these and still lead a miserable life. Many good people follow all of the rituals and ceremonies of their religion and nonetheless suffer the tortures of the damned. They expect misfortune, are afraid of God, and think that He's going to punish them. They worry about death, the devil, voodoo, the stars, disease, and the afterlife. They manifest problems because they're filling their subconscious with negative convictions.

Emerson wasn't interested in the rituals of the church, such as confession, baptism, or communion. In fact, he despised them. He didn't believe in Sunday school and forcing children to sit in a pew, answering questions against their will. He didn't believe that they were taught anything useful about God or life in this way. Instead of learning that the Divine Presence was within them, they were being instructed that God was out in space somewhere and that if they didn't do certain things, He would punish them. The church leaders said that if they were sinners, they might go to hell or be punished by a devil. Of course, this frightens the life out of children.

⊷✦⊶

Emerson didn't believe that it was possible to sin against God. He wrote: "There is a soul at the centre of nature, and over the will of every man, so that none of us can wrong the universe." Yes, the Life Principle is within every single one of us, even though we don't always recognize it. Turn to this Divine Source and say: "Infinite Intelligence leads and guides me in all my ways. It is a lamp unto my feet and a light upon my path. God reveals to me my true place in life." The response will come. If you're making an investment, affirm: "Infinite Intelligence guides me and reveals the answer to me. I follow the lead that comes clearly and distinctly into my conscious, reasoning mind." Follow through on the answer when it comes and don't discuss it with others, for then you'll have 50 thoughts coming into your mind. It's the first idea that flashes into your mind that's important.

⊷✦⊶

In Emerson's view, if you pray at an altar from a sense of duty, it's a profane act. In fact, there are no set rules for the spiritual life. You can pray under a tree, on an airplane, or driving along the road. He says that if you place yourself in the stream of Power that animates everything, the God Presence flows through you; and you're compelled to express right action, joy, and beauty. Yes, place yourself in the midst of the stream and say, "God flows through me as beauty, guidance, and harmony." On the other hand, when you oppose the law of mind, you experience hardship and problems.

⊷✦⊶

Emerson observed that everyone is unique because God never repeats Himself. Therefore, realize that God is flowing through you in a singular, extraordinary way. If you're a musician, Divine Spirit plays through you magnificently and stirs the soul. If you're open and receptive, you'll receive the music of the spheres and experience marvelous things in your life.

⊯✝⊯

Make yourself a clear channel for the Divine. If you have goodwill for all people, nothing can obstruct It. However, stress, strain, and anger will dam the flow and cause sickness and misfortune. If you're depressed and dejected, then you're clamping off the pipeline and the waters of love, light, and healing. Thoughts of criticism, bitterness, and spiritual pride also hold you back and impede your well-being and prosperity. Yes, take your foot off the hose, and the stream of good will course through your life.

⊯✝⊯

What truly belongs to you can't be withheld from you because you're a spiritual magnet and are in tune with the Infinite that animates all people. The good you desire will be yours when you're ready for it. As you contemplate the truth from the highest standpoint of God, marvelous things will happen. What's true of God becomes true of you.

⊯✝⊯

Every end is a beginning. Did you ever take a watch and observe the secondhand going around to the top of the dial? That's the end of a minute. Well, at that precise moment, another minute starts. This shows you that every end is a beginning. There can't be one without the other. This simple analogy shows us that loved ones who have passed on still live. They celebrate a new birthday in God and take on a fourth-dimensional body. Surely, we go from glory to glory, from strength to strength, and from wisdom to wisdom. There's no past or future—there's only the eternal now. Feel the Infinite Intelligence breathing through you, and you'll know what you should do.

⊸✛⊷

Both Emerson and Thomas Troward wrote that the Infinite is within us and that we're here to reproduce the light, love, truth, and beauty of God. That's how wonderful we are. Very few of us are fulfilling our potential, but we can always improve and release more and more of the Infinite. We can always meditate on wisdom, truth, and beauty.

⊸✛⊷

According to Emerson, there's really no competition in the universe because God can't compete with Himself. We're all parts of one stupendous Spirit. For example, Beethoven heard the music of the spheres within himself and rushed to the piano to compose. However, his works didn't prevent thousands of other musicians all over the world from creating their own beautiful music. Similarly, you may be doing $100,000 a year in sales. Another entrepreneur can have a new, creative idea and bring in $1 million annually, but he's not interfering with your profit. You can always decide to expand your own business. You're not interfering with anybody else or detracting from their love, wisdom, and inspiration when you decide to grow.

We're always evolving and outdoing ourselves because life itself is growth. There's no end to our glory, and good is always waiting to be expressed.

※✝※

God is a circle whose center is everywhere and His circumference nowhere. He's present in everything—in every blade of grass and every drop of water. The Living Spirit within is boundless and infinite. Never in eternity could you exhaust the wisdom and the glory that's in you.

In a Nutshell

Remember this theme of Emerson: *God walks and talks in you, and the entire world is simply God made manifest.*

If your mind is disturbed and you're mean to yourself, you can't get anywhere in meditation. Instead, go within to the silence, as Emerson did, and contemplate the truth of God from the highest standpoint. Realize that God is love and can't do anything unloving. When Divine compassion enters your soul, you'll automatically honor the Divinity in everybody.

Only ideas that are true heal, bless, inspire, elevate, and dignify your soul. Anything that instills fear into your mind, demeans you, or is contrary to love and harmony must be false. We need to be discerning to separate the chaff from the wheat and the false from the real.

The soul knows no deformity or pain. In Divine love, sorrow and grief disappear, peace casts out pain, and love dissolves hatred.

Whatever you claim to be true, you will experience because your subconscious manifests all of your thoughts. Therefore, don't squander your resources on destructive thinking.

The Infinite is within you, and you're here to reproduce the light, love, truth, and beauty of God. That's how wonderful you are. Very few of us are fulfilling our potential, but we can always improve. We can always release more and more of the Infinite and meditate on wisdom, truth, and beauty.

Chapter Ten

Mental and Spiritual Laws
in Light of Emerson (Part II)

*E*merson taught that we should realize that the Presence of God, which he called the *Over-Soul,* is within *ourselves.* He wrote: "Let us not rove; let us sit at home with the cause. Let us stun and astonish the intruding rabble of men and books and institutions, by a simple declaration of the divine fact. Bid the invaders take the shoes from off their feet, for God is here within. Let our simplicity judge them, and our docility to our own law demonstrate the poverty of nature and fortune beside our native riches."

Rise above into the Infinite dimension of Spirit. As you fill your mind with love, light, and truth, the past is forgotten and remembered no more. If you take a pail of dirty water and pour clean water into it, the moment comes when the water in the bucket is clear. Similarly, those who have a real hunger to change are transformed as they fill their soul with light. They can't repeat the same old mistakes because they're under Divine compulsion to do what's right.

᯾✞᯾

As we do unto others, so will it be done unto us by somebody somewhere. Both the good and the evil that do, we shall receive back in like measure. This doesn't mean that the same people we treat well or poorly will be the ones to reciprocate our behavior. No, it may be a complete stranger at some other time or place—someone who knows nothing of our previous actions—who will repay us grain for grain.

Emerson said that if we deceive, we'll also be deceived; and if we cheat, we'll also be cheated. The law of retribution is a cosmic law and is impersonal and unchanging. It's like gravity: It affects everyone equally and is never off duty. If people understood this better, there would be more integrity and justice in the world.

⊶✛⊷

Many people complain about ingratitude. Perhaps they help their relatives and friends or send a child to school and are hurt when they aren't offered appreciation. Don't bother looking for thanks; do what you feel is right and the Life Principle will repay you. When a policeman saves a man from drowning, the man may curse his rescuer. However, the officer did the right thing whether he's thanked for it or not.

Love doesn't look for a quid pro quo. For example, a mother doesn't tell her babies in the cradle, "Look, you've got to love me back." She just loves them unconditionally.

Don't resent others because you did something for them and they didn't return the favor. He Who gives all life and breath will always reward you. Of course, people who don't show appreciation do eventually suffer. They're only hurting themselves.

⊶✛⊷

Emerson discussed polarity in the universe. He said that we come into the world with an awareness of contrasts and opposites, including darkness and light, heat and cold, attraction and repulsion, sweet and sour, and so on. How would we know what joy is unless we'd shed tears of sorrow? How would we know what abundance is if we hadn't felt the pinch of poverty? We're here to reconcile the opposites and discover the Divinity that shapes our lives.

⁜

In India, many people believe in karma or the idea that if you commit sins in one life, you'll have to pay for them in another incarnation. However, when you have an intense desire to do good, you experience a transformation of the heart, and all karma is wiped out. That's the gospel. You can erase the past by feeding your subconscious with life-giving patterns. Even a heinous crime can be expunged, for love opens prison doors and sets the captives free.

However, superficial prayer won't suffice to fundamentally alter your character; it requires a strong realization of the power of God to wipe out the errors of the past. Once you realize the Presence within, you'll be compelled to be a good person because your subconscious assumptions and beliefs dictate all of your conscious actions. *Blessed are they who hunger and thirst after righteousness, for they shall be fed.*

⁜

If you've misused the principles of chemistry for 30 years, do they now hold a grudge against you and prevent you from using them correctly to create marvelous new compounds? Do the laws of mathematics resent you because you gave the wrong change to someone? Of course not! The minute you begin to add and subtract correctly, the past is forgotten. In the same way, your mind is a principle that doesn't nurse animosities. When you begin to think, feel, and act in a positive way, your subconscious automatically responds to conform to the new pattern in your conscious mind.

⻖✝⻖

In the Bible, we read about a man who was born blind. People came to Jesus and asked, "Did this man sin, or did his parents commit wrongdoings that caused him to be born without sight?" Jesus knew what they were thinking. In those days, they likely believed that the blind man must have committed crimes in a former life and was now being punished. Or they might have thought that the sins of his ancestors were being visited upon him. However, Jesus answered, "Neither this man nor his parents sinned, but that the works of God should be revealed in him. I must work the works of Him who sent Me while it is day; the night is coming when no one can work. As long as I am in the world, I am the light of the world."

Then Jesus said to the blind man, "Go wash in the pool of Siloam," which meant "Get rid of the false beliefs in your mind." The man did so and could then see perfectly.

This biblical story shows us that the Absolute doesn't judge or punish us for what we or our ancestors have done. As soon as we fill our mind with the truth and cast off misguided ideas, we'll also see clearly and experience great things in our lives.

⻖✝⻖

In the biblical parable of the workers in the vineyard, the laborers who were hired at the 11th hour received the same wages as those who'd begun working earlier. Similarly, some people learn about the law of mind late in life and immediately decide to use it to transform their existence. They may accomplish more in a few days or weeks than those who've been studying the truth for 40 years. There's no time or space in mind, and you can come in at the 11th hour and still be greatly rewarded. You might have led a frightful life, but now you can transform it.

The moment you change your conscious mind and begin to claim the good things of life—such as harmony, peace, and love—the law honors your claim. It makes no difference how long you've been in error or how you may have misused the law because Divine Spirit holds no grudges. People are forever condemning themselves, but once you've really changed, the past is forgotten. You're not punished for your mistakes; you learn from them.

❈

According to Emerson, nature compensates us for every "defect." For example, some people say, "How unfortunate it was for Helen Keller to be blind and deaf." On the contrary, she tuned in to the Infinite and walked in internal luminosity through the corridors of her mind. Look at what she gave! She lifted people up and inspired them. She walked with God and gave more to shut-ins and others than people with functioning eyes and ears.

Also consider John Milton, who wrote the epic poem *Paradise Lost*. He was blind, but he communed with the light of Infinite Spirit and gave a great work of literature to the world. As well, Beethoven was deaf yet brought forth magnificent music, and we're all blessed because he walked the earth. Yes, nature is absolutely just and eminently fair.

❈

I talked with a doctor in London. He'd been born into poverty, while his cousin had been born in a medieval palace to very rich parents who gave him private tutors and sent him to Oxford.

The doctor said that he sold newspapers, washed cars and windows, and did other menial labor so that he could earn money to pay for his medical studies. In time, he became a great surgeon. The cousin who'd been born with a silver spoon in his mouth, on the other hand, turned to alcohol and began running around with other men's wives. Tragically, his car went over an embankment, and he and the woman he was with were killed.

This story illustrates that as you sow in your mind, so shall you reap. One cousin had misused his mind, while the other had employed his brilliantly to create a wonderful life. You find examples like this all around the world. It makes no difference where or how you were born. You may have grown up in a ghetto, but you can rise out of it. You can become a great scientist like George Washington Carver by using your mind well.

⁂

Emerson wrote that some people who profess to be religious don't see that they close the door of heaven on themselves when they strive to shut others out. In fact, God doesn't exclude anybody. He's omnipresent and available to all people. He's always there in times of trouble. You should also strive to include everybody. If you reject somebody, you're rejecting yourself; and if you withhold something from another, you're withholding it from yourself. There's only one law, and no one has a monopoly on it. In Him, there's no male or female, and no Catholics, Protestants, or Hindus. God knows nothing about creeds, dogmas, or traditions, for He is Spirit. There's only the river of reality flowing on forever.

⁂

When you don't believe in loss or lack, you won't experience theft, which is a manifestation of your own belief in limitation. As Emerson noted: "No one steals from you unless you steal from yourself first." You may be robbing yourself of peace, harmony, joy, love, faith, and confidence. Instead, align yourself with the Infinite ocean of light and love. Your security rests in the invisible Presence and Power.

⁂

Avarice is an abnormal desire that stems from insecurity or the fear that there isn't enough to go around. That attitude of mind attracts lack and limitation. Greedy people are denying the Presence and Power of God within and are impoverishing themselves.

⇥✦⇤

Emerson said that nothing is hidden that isn't ultimately revealed. Therefore, don't fret over apparent injustice or evildoers. The mills of the gods grind slowly, but they grind exceedingly fine. The law is always fulfilled, and all evil destroys itself. You might say, "That man has murdered and robbed people, but his wife has three cars, his son goes to a private school, and they have a beautiful home."

Well, people who murder have killed something in themselves. They've strangled love, peace, harmony, and joy. They're denying the Life Principle and will experience guilt and fear. The law always metes out retribution, whether it's 5 or 20 years later. You may read in the newspaper that the murderer was imprisoned or that he died of a brain tumor. The Bible says: "Vengeance is Mine, and recompense; their foot shall slip in due time; for the day of their calamity is at hand. And the things to come hasten upon them."

⇥✦⇤

When World War II broke out, a woman read about a coming coffee shortage. Out of fear and avarice, she went around to all the stores and loaded up her car with coffee. In the evening, she went to church, and when she got back, burglars had taken all of the coffee and many other things besides.

When you covet something or fear not having enough, like this woman did, you're denying the Presence and Power of God within yourself. The movement of your thought attracts lack and limitation to you. Remember that God in the midst of you is guiding you now. When you see the truth, inequalities vanish.

⌖

In his essay, "Self-Reliance," Emerson wrote:

> Most men gamble with her [Fortune], and gain all, and lose
> all, as her wheel rolls. But do thou leave as unlawful these win-
> nings, and deal with Cause and Effect, the chancellors of God. In
> the Will work and acquire, and thou hast chained the wheel of
> Chance, and shalt sit hereafter out of fear from her rotations. A
> political victory, a rise of rents, the recovery of your sick, or the
> return of your absent friend, or some other favorable event, raises
> your spirits, and you think good days are preparing for you. Do
> not believe it. Nothing can bring you peace but yourself. Nothing
> can bring you peace but the triumph of principles.

Let us learn the principle of life: *Whatever you impress on your
subconscious is expressed on the screen of space as form, function, experience, and events.* You mold and fashion your own destiny, and
you answer your own prayers. It is done unto you as you believe.
If you think that you've been jinxed, you've imposed that hex on
yourself; and you'll attract lack, limitation, and misery.

⌖

The mass mind is operating in all of us, and we're all subject
to both the good and bad ideas it contains. If you're experiencing
any fear, doubt, worry, or anxiety, that's the mass mind thinking
in you. However, you can take action and prevent the mass mind
from dominating you. Will you go along with the herd, or are you
going to take charge of your own life?

Contemplate the truths of God from the highest standpoint,
as Emerson advises. Announce your conviction in Divine love and
believe in a God of goodness in the land of the living. Say, "I believe
in the peace of the Everlasting Being saturating my mind and my
heart, and I believe that wonders are happening in my life. Divine

love goes before me, making my path straight, joyous, and glorious." Charge your mental and spiritual batteries with your sincere belief every morning and night, and you'll neutralize and obliterate the negative patterns of the mass mind.

⋇

Emerson shows us that our essential nature is Divine Spirit. Self-reliance is, therefore, reliance on the Higher Self, which forever breathes and moves through us. We can rely on the Over-Soul that created the universe. It's the All-Wise, Eternal One that always responds to us and never fails. We can trust that.

You can say, "Divine love fills my soul," and meditate on the Infinite Presence for 15 minutes or half an hour. Unite with the One Power.

⋇

In "Self-Reliance," Emerson wrote: " There is a time in every man's education when he arrives at the conviction that envy is ignorance; that imitation is suicide; that he must take himself for better for worse as his portion . . . "

Of course envy is ignorance. If you're coveting somebody else's car, jewels, or promotion, you're denying that you can also have these things. You're saying, "That person has them, but I can't get them." Your thoughts are on lack and limitation, and you're impoverishing yourself—even if you don't realize what you're doing. However, you can go within to Spirit and claim your good. If you feel and believe it, Spirit will manifest it.

Emerson also mentioned the dangers of imitation. What's the use of copying someone? You're unique and extraordinary because God never repeats Himself. He has a special plan for you, and to tap into it, all you need to do is say, "God thinks, speaks, and acts through me. God creates through me, and I am inspired from On High."

⸺✦⸺

You're told that without faith, it's impossible to please God. You must first believe that God *is* and then seek Him diligently. When you're one with the Infinite Power, It becomes active and potent in your life. Nothing can oppose or thwart It.

If you claim your oneness with Infinite Intelligence, you're not being egotistical or aggressive—you're just exercising your natural dominion over your thoughts. God doesn't allow His work to be done by cowards, but only by those who are confident. Come into His presence singing. Come into His courts with praise.

⸺✦⸺

Societies everywhere conspire against the individuality of every one of their members. However, self-reliance is the opposite of conformity. It's relying on the Infinite Being within you—the All-Wise, Eternal One.

Are you conforming to the old traditions of your father and mother? Perhaps everything you believe is a lie. Have you ever asked yourself: *Where did my beliefs originate? Are they true? Are they logical? Are they scientific?* If they're contrary to the laws of nature, they must be absolutely false.

⸺✦⸺

People who accomplish great things must be nonconformists. For example, Henry Ford said, "We don't have to use horses and buggies," and he put the whole world on wheels. Thomas Edison insisted that we didn't have to rely on candles or oil lamps, and he decided to light up the planet with electric bulbs. All of the great religious teachers, including Jesus, Moses, Buddha, and Mohammed, were nonconformists who went against the thinking of the day. Are *you* an independent being? Are you thinking for yourself?

⅀⅏⅀

Emerson wrote: "Trust thyself: every heart beats to that iron string." Henry Brown, one of the teachers of New Thought in the early days, came across this passage when he lived in Nebraska at the close of the Civil War. Emerson's words touched his heart and changed his life. Brown said, "No longer am I afraid of some wrong-doing. I trust myself. I have desires, and my motivation is right. I say, 'I'm going to do this because the Absolute is in me, guiding me.' Why should I hesitate or be afraid?"

Come home to the truth like Henry Brown did, and you'll be transformed, too. Realize that the Absolutely Trustworthy One is in you, leading and helping you. Infinite Presence loves and cares for you. It's not arrogant or egotistical to claim this; rather, it's an indication of a healthy respect for the Divinity that created you. Contact the Power and Presence within you that knows and sees everything.

⅀⅏⅀

If all the words that are written and spoken about the Deity in all of the religions of the world were condensed into one sentence, it would come down to this simple, simple truth: *Trust the Absolute in your own heart.* If you don't trust or love yourself, you can't care for anybody. If a man doesn't love himself, he can't love his wife even if he goes through the motions. Loving someone is wishing him or her to be happy, joyous, and free. It's exalting the God in the other.

⅀⅏⅀

Emerson criticized those who wanted to take care of people thousands of miles away while neglecting their family and community. He wrote: "Love afar is spite at home." Consider your own life.

Are you at peace with your wife, your husband, and your children? Is there love, harmony, and peace in your home? Do you love your neighbor? Do you radiate compassion and goodwill at work? Are you exalting God in the midst of you? The answers to these questions will be very telling.

⊷✛⊶

Many people have embraced a system of religious dogma, but they have no workable faith, and their lives are chaotic. Others may not belong to any church at all; but they lead marvelous lives, are full of love and goodwill, are doing constructive work for the neighborhood, and have wonderful families. They practice the golden rule, or the law of love. They have a practical faith that's expressed in their business, their home life, and their relationship with the community.

⊷✛⊶

One of life's primary lessons is that all boys and girls must learn to stand on their own two feet. Don't rob them of their chance to discover their Divinity or encounter difficulties, for that's the way they learn about their strength. The joy is in overcoming. They're here to face their problems just the same as you did, and they need to do so as independently as possible.

If you give them too much help, they soon learn that relying on others is easier than self-propulsion, and they become whiners and "leaners." We have them all over the place. The constant provision of money, food, and that sort of thing fosters a false view and is destructive to their developing characters. It really is. You should instead help others help *themselves*. Be very careful how you do it, and don't take away their chance to discover their Divinity within.

꽃

All healing is spiritual. If you had faith in God and were walking in the consciousness of love, faith, and harmony at all times, you'd never get sick. It's as simple as that. If you do become ill, go to a doctor as soon as you can and pray, and you should see results right away.

꽃

No one has the right to invade your life and tell you how you should feed your children, the way you should think, what religion you should belong to, how you should clothe yourself, or what color you should paint your house. In addition, no one should expect you to cater to their shortcomings, delinquencies, laziness, and neuroses. Be true to your own ideals, and don't let anyone sidetrack you.

Trust the silent Presence within you and ask for Divine guidance. Never depart from the truth within yourself; and make your own decisions regarding money, morals, friendship, and everything else. Realize as Emerson taught that nothing will give you peace but the triumph of principles. As Shakespeare wrote: "To thine own self be true, and it must follow, as the night the day, thou canst not then be false to any man."

In a Nutshell

As we think, speak, and act toward others, so others will act toward us. What we give out will come back to us, and everything that we do to others will sooner or later be done to us by somebody somewhere.

The moment you change your conscious mind and begin to claim the good things of life—such as harmony, peace, and love—the law honors your claim.

People are forever being self-critical and condemning themselves, but, in fact, your subconscious always forgives. It makes no difference how long you've been in error or how you may have misused the law. It doesn't hold anything against you. Once you've really changed, the past is forgotten and remembered no more. You're not punished for your mistakes; you learn through them.

What you give out will always be returned to you. Therefore, sent out love, peace, and harmony. Radiate goodwill and give a transfusion of faith and confidence to all those around you.

Announce your conviction in Divine love and the goodness of God in the land of the living. Say, "I believe in the peace of the Everlasting Being saturating my mind and my heart; I believe that wonders are happening in my life and that Divine love goes before me, making my path straight, joyous, and glorious." Every morning and night, charge your mental and spiritual batteries with that belief, and you'll neutralize and obliterate the negative patterns of the mass mind.

No one has the right to invade your life and tell you how you should feed your children, the way you should think, what religion you should belong to, how you should clothe yourself, or what color you should paint your house. In addition, no one has the right to expect you to cater to their shortcomings, delinquencies, laziness, and neuroses.

Are you thinking for yourself? Do you trust yourself? If you don't trust or love yourself, you can't care for anybody. Loving someone is wishing him or her to be happy, joyous, and free. It's exalting the God in the other.

Biography of Joseph Murphy

*J*oseph Murphy was born on May 20, 1898, in a small town in the County of Cork, Ireland. His father, Denis Murphy, was a deacon and professor at the National School of Ireland, a Jesuit facility. His mother, Ellen, née Connelly, was a housewife, who later gave birth to another son, John, and a daughter, Catherine.

Joseph was brought up in a strict Catholic household. His father was quite devout and, indeed, was one of the few lay professors who taught Jesuit seminarians. He had a broad knowledge of many subjects and developed in his son the desire to study and learn.

Ireland at that time was suffering from one of its many economic depressions, and many families were starving. Although Denis Murphy was steadily employed, his income was barely enough to sustain the family.

Young Joseph was enrolled in the National School and was a brilliant student. He was encouraged to study for the priesthood and was accepted as a Jesuit seminarian. However, by the time he reached his late teen years, he began to question the Catholic orthodoxy of the Jesuits, and he withdrew from the seminary. Since his goal was to explore new ideas and gain new experiences —a goal he couldn't pursue in Catholic-dominated Ireland—he left his family to go to America.

He arrived at the Ellis Island Immigration Center with only $5 in his pocket. His first project was to find a place to live. He was fortunate to locate a rooming house where he shared a room with a pharmacist who worked in a local drugstore.

Joseph's knowledge of English was minimal, as Gaelic was spoken both in his home and at school, so like most Irish immigrants, Joseph worked as a day laborer, earning enough to keep himself fed and housed.

He and his roommate became good friends, and when a job opened up at the drugstore where his friend worked, he was hired to be an assistant to the pharmacist. He immediately enrolled in a school to study pharmacy. With his keen mind and desire to learn, it didn't take long before Joseph passed the qualification exams and became a full-fledged pharmacist. He now made enough money to rent his own apartment. After a few years, he purchased the drugstore, and for the next few years ran a successful business.

When the United States entered World War II, Joseph enlisted in the Army and was assigned to work as a pharmacist in the medical unit of the 88th Infantry Division. At that time, he renewed his interest in religion and began to read extensively about various spiritual beliefs. After his discharge from the Army, he chose not to return to his career in pharmacy. He traveled extensively, taking courses in several universities both in the United States and abroad.

From his studies, Joseph became enraptured with the various Asian religions and went to India to learn about them in depth. He studied all of the major faiths and their histories. He extended these studies to the great philosophers from ancient times until the present.

Although he studied with some of the most intelligent and farsighted professors, the one person who most influenced Joseph was Dr. Thomas Troward, who was a judge as well as a philosopher, doctor, and professor. Judge Troward became Joseph's mentor and introduced him to the study of philosophy, theology, and law as well as mysticism and the Masonic order. Joseph became an active member of this order, and over the years rose in the Masonic ranks to the 32nd degree in the Scottish Rite.

Upon his return to the United States, Joseph chose to become a minister and bring his broad knowledge to the public. As his

concept of Christianity was not traditional and indeed ran coun-
ter to most of the Christian denominations, he founded his own
church in Los Angeles. He attracted a small number of congregants,
but it did not take long for his message of optimism and hope
rather than the "sin-and-damnation" sermons of so many ministers to attract many men and women to his church.

Dr. Joseph Murphy was a proponent of the New Thought
movement. This movement was developed in the late 19th and
early 20th centuries by many philosophers and deep thinkers who
studied this phenomenon and preached, wrote, and practiced a
new way of looking at life. By combining a metaphysical, spiritual,
and pragmatic approach to the way we think and live, they uncovered the secret of attaining what we truly desire.

The proponents of the New Thought movement preached a
new idea of life that is based on practical, spiritual principles that
we can all use to enrich our lives and create perfect results. We can
do these things only as we have found the law and worked out
the understanding of the law, which God seems to have written in
riddles in the past.

Of course, Dr. Murphy wasn't the only minister to preach
this positive message. Several churches, whose ministers and congregants were influenced by the New Thought movement, were
founded and developed in the decades following World War II.
The Church of Religious Science, Unity Church, and other places
of worship preach philosophies similar to this. Dr. Murphy named
his organization The Church of Divine Science. He often shared
platforms, conducted joint programs with his like-minded col-
leagues, and trained other men and women to join his ministry.

Over the years, other churches joined with him in developing an organization called the Federation of Divine Science, which
serves as an umbrella for all Divine Science churches. Each of the
Divine Science church leaders continues to push for more education, and Dr. Murphy was one of the leaders who supported the
creation of the Divine Science School in St. Louis, Missouri, to

train new ministers and provide ongoing education for both ministers and congregants.

The annual meeting of the Divine Science ministers was a must to attend, and Dr. Murphy was a featured speaker at this event. He encouraged the participants to study and continue to learn, particularly about the importance of the subconscious mind.

Over the next few years, Murphy's local Church of Divine Science grew so large that his building was too small to hold them. He rented The Wilshire Ebell Theater, a former movie theater. His services were so well attended that even this venue could not always accommodate all who wished to attend. Classes conducted by Dr. Murphy and his staff supplemented his Sunday services that were attended by 1,300 to 1,500 people. Seminars and lectures were held most days and evenings. The church remained at the Wilshire Ebell Theater in Los Angeles until 1976, when it moved to a new location in Laguna Hills, California.

To reach the vast numbers of people who wanted to hear his message, Dr. Murphy also created a weekly radio talk show, which eventually reached an audience of over a million listeners. Many of his followers suggested that he tape his lectures and radio programs. He was at first reluctant to do so, but agreed to experiment. His radio programs were recorded on extra-large 78-rpm discs, a common practice at that time. He had six cassettes made from one of these discs and placed them on the information table in the lobby of the Wilshire Ebell Theater. They sold out the first hour. This started a new venture. His tapes of his lectures explaining biblical texts, and providing meditations and prayers for his listeners, were not only sold in his church, but in other churches and bookstores and via mail order.

As the church grew, Dr. Murphy added a staff of professional and administrative personnel to assist him in the many programs in which he was involved and in researching and preparing his first books. One of the most effective members of his staff was his administrative secretary, Dr. Jean Wright. Their working

relationship developed into a romance, and they were married—
a lifelong partnership that enriched both of their lives.

At this time (the 1950s), there were very few major publishers of spiritually inspired material. The Murphys located some
small publishers in the Los Angeles area, and worked with them
to produce a series of small books (often 30 to 50 pages printed in
pamphlet form) that were sold, mostly in churches, from $1.50
to $3.00 per book. When the orders for these books increased to
the point where they required second and third printings, major
publishers recognized that there was a market for such books and
added them to their catalogs.

Dr. Murphy became well known outside of the Los Angeles
area as a result of his books, tapes, and radio broadcasts, and was
invited to lecture all over the country. He did not limit his lectures
to religious matters, but spoke on the historical values of life, the
art of wholesome living, and the teachings of great philosophers—
from both Eastern and Western cultures.

Since Dr. Murphy had never learned to drive, he had to arrange
for somebody to drive him to the various places where he was
invited to lecture in his very busy schedule. One of Jean's functions as his administrative secretary and later his wife was to plan
his assignments and arrange for trains or flights, airport pickups,
hotel accommodations, and all the other details of the trips.

The Murphys traveled frequently to many countries around
the world. One of his favorite working vacations was to hold seminars on cruise ships. These trips lasted a week or more and would
take him to many countries around the world. In his lectures, he
emphasized the importance of understanding the power of the
subconscious mind and the life principles based on belief in the
one God, the "I AM."

One of Dr. Murphy's most rewarding activities was speaking
to the inmates at many prisons. Many ex-convicts wrote him over
the years, telling him how his words had truly turned their lives
around and inspired them to live spiritual and meaningful lives.

Dr. Murphy's pamphlet-sized books were so popular that he began to expand them into more detailed and longer works. His wife gave us some insight into his manner and method of writing. She reported that he wrote his manuscripts on a tablet and pressed so hard on his pencil or pen that you could read the imprint on the next page. He seemed to be in a trance while writing. He would remain in his office for four to six hours without disturbance until he stopped and said that was enough for the day. Each day was the same. He never went back into the office again until the next morning to finish what he'd started. He took no food or drink while he was working, He was just alone with his thoughts and his huge library of books, to which he referred from time to time. His wife sheltered him from visitors and calls and took care of church business and other activities.

Dr. Murphy was always looking for simple ways to discuss the issues and to elaborate on points. He chose some of his lectures to present on cassettes, records, or CDs, as technologies developed in the audio field.

His entire collection of CDs and cassettes are tools that can be used for most problems that individuals encounter in life. His basic theme is that the solution to problems lies within you. Outside elements cannot change your thinking. That is, your mind is your own. To live a better life, it's your mind, not outside circumstances, that you must change. You create your own destiny. The power of change is in your mind, and by using the power of your subconscious mind, you can make changes for the better.

Dr. Murphy wrote more than 30 books. His most famous work, *The Power of the Unconscious Mind,* which was first published in 1963, became an immediate bestseller. It was acclaimed as one of the best self-help guides ever written. Millions of copies have been sold and continue to be sold all over the world.

Among some of his other best-selling books were *Telepsychics— The Magic Power of Perfect Living, The Amazing Laws of Cosmic Mind, Secrets of the I-Ching, The Miracle of Mind Dynamics, Your Infinite Power to Be Rich,* and *The Cosmic Power Within You.*

Dr. Murphy died in December 1981; and his wife, Dr. Jean Murphy, continued his ministry after his death. In a lecture she gave in 1986, quoting her late husband, she reiterated his philosophy:

> I want to teach men and women of their Divine Origin, and the powers pregnant within them. I want to inform that this power is within and that they are their own saviors and capable of achieving their own salvation. This is the message of the Bible and nine-tenths of our confusion today is due to wrongful, literal interpretation of the life-transforming truths offered in it.
>
> I want to reach the majority, the man on the street, the woman overburdened with duty and suppression of her talents and abilities. I want to help others at every stage or level of consciousness to learn of the wonders within.

She said of her husband: "He was a practical mystic, possessed by the intellect of a scholar, the mind of a successful executive, the heart of the poet." His message summed up was: "You are the king, the ruler of your world, for you are one with God."

Notes

Notes

Notes

Notes

Notes

Notes

Notes

Notes

Notes

Notes

Notes

Notes

Hay House Titles of Related Interest

CALM: *A Proven Four-Step Process Designed Specifically for Women Who Worry,* by Denise Marek

THE POWER OF A SINGLE THOUGHT: *How to Initiate Major Life Changes from the Quiet of Your Mind* (book-with-CD), revised and edited by Gay Hendricks and Debbie DeVoe

THE POWER OF INTENTION: *Learning to Co-create Your World Your Way,* by Dr. Wayne W. Dyer

10 STEPS TO TAKE CHARGE OF YOUR EMOTIONAL LIFE: *Overcoming Anxiety, Distress, and Depression Through Whole-Person Healing,* by Eve A. Wood, M.D.

WHAT TO DO WHEN YOU DON'T KNOW WHAT TO DO: *Common Horse Sense,* by Wyatt Webb

꙾✛꙾

All of the above are available at your local bookstore, or may be ordered by visiting Hay House (see last page).

꙾✛꙾

☙✦❧

We hope you enjoyed this Hay House book.
If you'd like to receive a free catalog featuring additional
Hay House books and products, or if you'd like information
about the Hay Foundation, please contact:

Hay House, Inc.
P.O. Box 5100
Carlsbad, CA 92018-5100

(760) 431-7695 or (800) 654-5126
(760) 431-6948 (fax) or (800) 650-5115 (fax)
www.hayhouse.com® • www.hayfoundation.org

☙✦❧

Published and distributed in Australia by: Hay House Australia Pty.
Ltd., 18/36 Ralph St., Alexandria NSW 2015 • *Phone:* 612-9669-4299
Fax: 612-9669-4144 • www.hayhouse.com.au

Published and distributed in the United Kingdom by:
Hay House UK, Ltd., 292B Kensal Rd., London W10 5BE • *Phone:*
44-20-8962-1230 • *Fax:* 44-20-8962-1239 • www.hayhouse.co.uk

Published and distributed in the Republic of South Africa by:
Hay House SA (Pty), Ltd., P.O. Box 990, Witkoppen 2068 • *Phone/Fax:*
27-11-467-8904 • orders@psdprom.co.za • www.hayhouse.co.za

Published in India by: Hay House Publishers India, Muskaan
Complex, Plot No. 3, B-2, Vasant Kunj, New Delhi 110 070 • *Phone:*
91-11-4176-1620 • *Fax:* 91-11-4176-1630 • www.hayhouse.co.in

Distributed in Canada by: Raincoast, 9050 Shaughnessy St.,
Vancouver, B.C. V6P 6E5 • *Phone:* (604) 323-7100
Fax: (604) 323-2600 • www.raincoast.com

☙✦❧

Tune in to **HayHouseRadio.com**® for the best in inspirational
talk radio featuring top Hay House authors! And, sign up via the
Hay House USA Website to receive the Hay House online newsletter
and stay informed about what's going on with your favorite authors.
You'll receive bimonthly announcements about Discounts and Offers,
Special Events, Product Highlights, Free Excerpts, Giveaways, and more!
www.hayhouse.com®